Advertising vs. Marketing:
The Ethical Challenge

by

Ileen E. Kelly

ISBN: 1-58112-266-7

DISSERTATION.COM

Boca Raton, Florida
USA • 2005

Advertising vs. Marketing: The Ethical Challenge

Dissertation.com
Boca Raton, Florida
USA • 2005

ISBN: 1-58112- 266-7

ADVERTISING vs. MARKETING

THE ETHICAL CHALLENGE

by

Dr. Ileen E. Kelly, Ph.D.

Chicago, IL. 2004

ACKNOWLEDGEMENTS

I would like to thank my sister Rachel Burke, my brother and sister in-law Rev. Richard and Sharon Kelly; my niece and nephews Raven Burke, Richard D. Kelly III and Cody M. Kelly for all their support as I embarked upon this journey to reach my academic goal.   To my parents Richard D. and Anna L. Kelly who both left this earth much to early,   but, you engrained in all your children the importance of letting God lead the way. Joan and James Shelton who encouraged my personal and career goals. Barbara Campbell, you carried me when I could not stand. Family, I can honestly say that with your help and support the journey has been as wonderful as reaching my destination…

To all of my friends and colleagues for your assistance with research collection, editing and critiquing; to Kim Mann, Ph.D., Chicago State University for your truthful guidance and support in the writing and Michele Allen for reminding me to enjoy life as well.

Without all of you, this project would not have been completed.

Cover Designed by: Arnie "Lil Bill" Nelson, Oak Forest, IL

Spiritual Support: Robert Iannotti; Marie Smith; and Jack Whisler.

TABLE OF CONTENTS

ABSTRACT

Multiple business models have been presented each reflecting their strengths and weaknesses. One models demonstrate consumer purchase behavior. The second model demonstrates marketing strategies. A third model demonstrates the use of various advertising vehicles and the last model demonstrates the human aspect that combines salesmanship and management leadership with ethical business conduct.

This researcher found a multitude of   articles, books, journals, and websites on each singular topic and recognized the need for these models to merge.   Based on the readings, we'll review the pros and cons of ethics that favor the end results from which decisions are judged as ethical, versus the ethics that require the means to be ethical as well.

It may seems antithetical, but the more narrowly you define your target market while practicing both the company business code and your personal ethics code establishes a strong a reputation.

Many 4D developers have built successful businesses focussing on small- to mid-size companies. Large companies tend to have their own development staff in house.

CHAPTER 1

INTRODUCTION

Consideration of the moral dimension of marketing has increased significantly in recent years. Areas of literature such as marketing ethics have experienced rapid development since their emergence (or re-emergence) in the 1980s; new forms of behavior such as ethical consumerism and ethical and theories such as macro marketing, social marketing and the societal marketing concept have become firmly established constituents of marketing though. It would be wrong, however, to assume that these new areas of interest represent evidence of moral issues entering marketing thought for as long as marketing has existed as a distinct field in itself, and since then there have been a number of waves of interest in morality. Marketing is therefore an extraordinarily rich field in which to study morality.

There have long been moral criticisms of marketing, even from before marketing came into being as a field of study. As an academic enquiry, these criticisms began to be formalized in the late 1950s, and since the 1960s their development has become more sophisticated and extensive. I should like to analyze this literature by dividing the criticisms into three main groups. First, we have those that question the functioning of the marketing system, i.e. they seek to throw doubt upon the consumer sovereignty model of marketing.

Second, there are those that question the impact of marketing on society, i.e.

they seek to illustrate the socially undesirable results of marketing. Third,

there are those criticisms that explore incidences of unethical marketing, i.e.

they question the actual manner in which marketing is conducted. Morality

has been used to explore the problems and pitfalls of marketing theory and

practice.

The moral basis of marketing theory is based upon the notion of the

sovereign consumer, and it is perhaps unsurprising that both marketing

theory and practice are replete with the discourse of consumer sovereignty.

Most common definitions of marketing and the marketing concept tend to be

predicated on the consumer sovereignty mode, with emphasis firmly placed

on the need for 'customer orientation', ' customer focus', 'customer-driven

strategies', or some such version of what is essentially an 'outside-in

perspective'. The following, taken from one popular text book (Kotler et al.

1996), is indicative of most definitions of the marketing concept, and is

explicit in its promotion of Galbraith's (1972) accepted sequence:

The marketing concept holds that achieving organizational goals

depends on determining the needs and wants of target markets and

delivering the desired satisfactions more effective and efficient than

competitors. (Kotler et al. 1996:15)

The discourse of consumer sovereignty has by now permeated beyond marketing into a broad range of theoretical and practical arenas of management in contemporary organizations and organizational theory (Du Gay and Salaman 1992). It is however, based on two critical assumptions: 1) that needs originate from the consumer; and 2) that firms identify and act upon the needs when translated into consumer demand. Both of these have been criticized as empirically inaccurate.

The publication "The Affluent Society in 1958 provided an early, important and influential moral critique of marketing. It argues that firms generate rather than satisfy consumer needs, claiming that the industrial system had assumed sufficient size and power to render the consumer helpless in deciding what and how much is produced. This represented the 'revised sequence' – a categorical denial of the 'accepted sequence' of consumer sovereignty, which accords power in the economic system to the individual. Modern industrialized countries were effectively planned economies, ruled over by large self-serving corporations with little regard for the public interest. The massive expenditures on marketing were in fact cited by Galbraith as evidence for want creation on a huge scale. Also in the late 1950s, Packards' populist work, 'The Hidden Persuaders, brought moral concerns about the manipulation of consumer need through marketing to a still wider audience. With his stylistic mixture of conspiracy theory and 'pop' psychology, Packard sought to reveal how the 'depth

men' of consumer research callously turned the hidden urges and

frustrations of innocent consumers into blind desires for unnecessary and

unwanted products.

Baudrillard (1981, 1997) develops these ideas, claiming too that 'the

freedom and sovereignty of the consumer are mystification pure and

simple. Where he departs from Galbraith, however, is in his denial that if

consumers needs are created by marketing, they can be categorized as

'flase' or artificial', compared with underlying 'real' or 'natural' needs. He

proclaims that, in terms of the activities of consumption, there can be no

distinction, because consumers do not consume for use value or

exchange value, but for 'sign value'. Hence, all consumption is drive by a

single basic force which is 'the logic of social differentiation', i.e. the need

to distinguish oneself through the purchase and use of consumer goods.

The important unit of analysis is not individual need, but the system of

needs; and it is the system of needs that is the product of the system of

production.

Marketing then might not so much be regarded as creating need for

individual products, but rather, in aggregate, as contributing to the

capitalist culture, which emphasizes and rewards material accumulation.

In terms of consumer sovereignty though, the question of the origin of consumer need remains problematic – a point occasionally, though rarely, acknowledged in marketing textbooks. However, even if it could be argued that needs were objective and existing prior to consumption, for consumer sovereignty to be upheld, they would have to be duly acted upon by companies (Smith 1990; Dixon 1992; Knights et al. 1994). Smith (1990) however sets out the position that only under perfect competition will firms be passive to the demands of consumers. In practice, he suggests, this assumption clearly does not hold and therefore firms are likely to have discretionary power within the market (see also Galbraith 1977). It is this then that perverts the connection between consumer sovereignty and the marketing concept: consumer sovereignty presupposes the firm as passive whereas the marketing concept presupposes an active, strategic role for the firm (Smith 1990; Dixon 1992). Leading marketing academics such as Kotler explicitly acknowledge that marketing involves the firm not so much in responding to demand but in managing it:

> Marketing management seeks to affect the level, timing and nature of demand in a way that helps the organization achieves its objectives.

Simply put, marketing management is demand management. (Kotler et)

1.1 Statement of the Problem

The problem is to figure out what is morally relevant about marketing itself? Or what is morally relevant about particular marketing practices? These two questions have occupied marketing scholars and various critics of marketing throughout the development of marketing and its practice. Let's explore both, including not only the moral criticisms of marketing, but also the various lines of moral defense that have been forthcoming from marketing practitioners and academics.

1.2 Impact of Marketing on Society

Even if it could be argued that the consumer was fully sovereign in the economy, this would not necessarily provide a moral justification for traditional marketing theory. The marketing concept is concerned with marrying individual customer satisfaction with the firm profitability. This does not necessarily mean that social good is maximized. The consumption decision is an inherently individual one, where we seek to satisfy our own immediate needs and desires. For the most part, social concerns are not a significant force in our consumption decisions, since these are essentially about long-term, shared aspects of our lives. We might then distinguish between our concerns as consumers (what we want for ourselves) and our concerns as citizens (what we want for everyone).

1.3 Purpose of the Study

The purpose of this study is to develop a model for Business Ethics that will lead socially responsible businesses to operate responsibly towards the consumer. Its mission is to promote ethical business practices, serve the growing community of professionals striving to live and work in responsible ways, and create a financially healthy company in the process.

1.4 Importance of the Study

Advertising is constantly bombarded by criticism. It is accused of encouraging materialism and consumption, of stereotyping, of causing people to purchase items for which they have no need, of taking advantage of children, of manipulating consumer behavior, using sex to sell, and generally contributing to the downfall of our social system. Critics of advertising abound. Barely a week goes by without some advertisement or campaign, or the ad industry, being the focal point of some controversy. There even are web sites dedicated to criticizing various aspects of advertising.

To illustrate some of the many attacks on advertising, this researcher has compiled a list of recent examples that have appeared in recent magazines and newspapers.   This is *far* from being an exhaustive list. It is intended merely to provide you with some ideas about how the public-at-large perceives advertising, and to give you a sense of the many legal and ethical problems inherent in the advertising profession.

1.5 Scope of the Study

This study focuses on two targets, "Body Imaging" and the "Youth Market". Both are multi-billion dollar markets targeting both high and low self-esteem of consumers.

Diet and supplement industries are filled with corrupt marketing vultures that are getting rich by preying on your fears, hopes and aspirations. Unfortunately, there's been no way of protecting yourself from becoming a victim of these ruthless marketing practices. In the year 2002, Americans spent nearly $35.3 BILLION on diets and weight loss products! According to the Nutrition Business Journal, the supplement industry reached an all time high of $16.1 billion in sales in the year 2002. 1,000 different manufacturers produce about 20,000 different products, which are consumed by 100 million people! With billions at stake, these greedy supplement and weight loss companies will tell you anything through strategic advertising and marketing to get you to buy their products. They'll even lie right to your face! And the fact that the industry is so loosely regulated allows them to get away with it. Now that the prevalence of obesity in the United states has reached what health officials view as epidemic proportions, Americans are becoming more familiar with the consequences and so many are being victimized by high pressure marketing and advertising.

- **Analyze the current situation of demand and supply to a weight challenged and fitness conscience society**
- **Provide estimates in the growth of the fitness facilities across the country;**
- **Identify marketing opportunities for organic/natural supplements developed and developing in this country**
- **Identify the constraints needed to overcome marketers grip on a fearful society**

Advertising and Marketing to the youth market has been spiraling upward in the past two decades. In 2001 US advertising expenditures topped $230 billion, more than double the $105.97 billion spent in 1980. Given that the 2000 Census reports 105 million households in America, this means that advertisers spend, an average of $2,190 per year to reach one household.

The Department of Nutrition and Food Studies at New York University, estimates that $13 billion a year is spent marketing to American children – by the food and drink industries alone. Food Advertising makes up about half of all the advertising aimed at kids. Older kids, 12-19 spent a record $155 billion of their own money in 2001, up from $63 billion three years prior. In the 1960's children influenced about

$5 billion of their parents' purchases. By 1984 that figure increased the-fold to $50 billion. By 1997 it tripled to $188 billion. James McNeal, a kids marketing expert's estimates those expenditures in 2002 exceeded $500 billion. (Kids and Commercialism, 2003).

Kids are glued to the television, and are bombarded by commercials. It's estimated with the increase in cable specific viewer audience, the average child sees more than 20,000 commercials every year – that work out to at least 55 commercials per day. Top that with companion marketing, sponsorships, and access marketing (example: kiosk soda and snack machines in schools) manufacturers are creating brand-conscious babies to grow into consumers.

- **Review the top 5 manufacturers that target the teen dollar**
- **Analyze the current situation of demand and supply to a peer pressured society;**

- **Review estimates in the growth of teen spending**

- **Identify marketing opportunities used to capitalize on branding to the youth market**

- **Define strategy options for regulating marketing activity toward the youth market**

1.6 Methodology

Early in the first Reagan administration, Robert Heilbroner, (Ethics & Manipulation, 1997), critiqued supply-side economics in the New York Review of Books. One of his themes was capitalism's moral instability. According to Heilbroner, capitalism displaces traditional values and instills commercial ones in their stead. The main culprit in this unhealthy process, he thought, is advertising.

"If I were asked to name the deadliest subversive force within capitalism- the single greatest source of its waning morality – I should without hesitation name advertising. How else should one identify a force that debases language, drains thought, and undoes dignity? If the barrage of advertising, unchanged its tone and texture, were devoted to some other purpose-say the exaltation of the public sector-it would be recognized in a moment for the corrosive element that it is. But as the voice of the private sector it escapes this startled notice."

To analyze the ethics of advertising and marketing in this study the following approach was adopted. First, relevant literature, publications, newspaper articles, trade publications and studies were highlighted for in-depth information on current models of marketing specifically youth marketing and body image. Specifically eating and drinking habits along with the introduction of high tech. Second, Analyze key players approach these two markets including the soft drink and fast food industry. Reviewing recent surveys sourced from Gallup Chicago Media Usage and Consumer Behavior Poll, 2002; Audit Bureau of Circulations Annual Audit 2002; Audit Bureau of Circulations fast-fax, March 2003.

- The Gallup Poll of Media Usage and Consumer Behavior is one of the industry's leading research firms, the Gallup Organization has build a solid reputation for delivering reliable market statistics.

- Gallup continuously conducts comprehensive media usage and consumer behavior studies.

- Respondents are interviewed via telephone and through an extensive mail survey

- Information is available once a year

- A telephone survey collects respondents and household

  demographics, newspaper readership, radio listening,

  consumer purchasing habits.

- As many as 14 call attempts may be made to identify and contact

  eligible respondents.

- The mail survey is sent to all telephone respondents who give

  their name and address. This survey collects respondent

  and household consumer behavior patterns.

Audit Bureau of Circulations ("ABC") Circulation Reports:

- ABC was formed in 1914 by a group of advertisers, advertising
  agencies and newspaper publishers that joined together in an
  effort to set "ground rules" for circulation accounting. ABC was
  created to enforce those rules and to provide published reports

of verified circulation data to the buyers and sellers of print advertising space.

- ABC Publisher's Statement – Un-audited statement of circulation submitted by daily and weekly members of ABC twice a year, once in March and again in September. Shows print publications designated market.

GRPs/TRPs

■ **Based on objective third party research in the marketplace**

Service	Media	Accepted?	Used?	For
MRI/ Simmons	All	Yes	Yes	Planning (National)
Gallup/ Scarborough	All	Yes	Yes	Planning (Local)
Nielsen	TV	Yes	Yes	Buying
Arbitron	Radio	Yes	Yes	Buying

Lastly, the information obtained from Strategic Marketing reports will be reviewed and processed and weighed against information obtained from literature and other sources.

First hypothesis: There is a difference between ethical perceptions of predatory manufacturers vs. consumer confidence. A review of current consumer news and reports supports this assumption.

Second hypothesis: Existing advertising/marketing paradigms have been manipulated to suit the bottom-line revenue goals of manufacturers capitalizing on the fears and low self esteem of many consumers.

Remarks

The reader should keep in mind that the data provided in this publication are estimates, based on information obtained from market sources six month to 2 years old. The economic climate changes daily, particularly because of the current effects if the war in Iraq, unemployment; outsourcing, etc. The basic data needed to conclude this study is sufficient.

Definition of Terms

These terms are used throughout the study.

Ad Hoc Research: marketing research, which is designed to meet a particular issue usually on behalf of one client or company. Ad hoc research is conducted when there is insufficient existing research within the marketing information system to answer all the questions.

Advertising: process of information or persuasion of members of a particular target market or audience by placement of announcements and information in any of the mass media about products, services, organizations or ideas.

Advertising Campaign: group of commercials, advertisements, and other promotional material/activities used during a given period as part of a structured advertising plan.

Advertising Effectiveness: assessment of the extent to which specific advertisements/campaigns meet the objectives intended. Wide array of measurements are available, e.g. inquiry, recall, market tests. They include: Recall of ads, attitudes towards the advertising, persuasiveness/impact on current sales level etc.

Advertising Media: the various mass media that can be used to carry advertising messages to actual or potential audiences or target markets. These media include newspapers, magazines, direct mail advertising, Yellow Pages, radio, TV, outdoor advertising, transit advertising etc.

Advertising Objective: statement to define specific goals that should be accomplished by advertising activities e.g. products to be sold; number of trial purchasers, level of awareness of a message etc.

Advertorial: advertisement designed to give the appearance of editorial.

Advisory Board: small, closed meeting of worldwide, leading experts that provides full and frank advice on specific issues

Below the Line Advertising: term used in former times to incorporate medical scientific communications for approved drugs, e.g. educational materials. Less overt than above-the-line advertising. Have different connotations in a non-pharmaceutical context.

Benchmarking: assessing performance, usually of a company, but also of a product against acknowledged leaders in different fields of activity (e.g. production/marketing/finance etc.).

Bench Mark: see Base Line.

Benefit Segmentation: the division of a market according to the benefits that customers want from the product.

Brand: a set of unique and often intangible 'values' associated with a product or group of products, creating an aura, which transcends physical features, and resulting in much more than a commodity.

Brand Aid: system of models for determining the marketing mix for a specific brand.

Brand Awareness: extent to which a brand or brand name is recognized by potential customers, and correctly associated with the product offering and values in question.

Brand Equity: the goodwill associated with a brand name, which adds tangible value to a company through the resulting higher profits and sales.

Brand Extension: type of branding in which a firm uses one of its existing brand names as part of a brand for an improved or new product that is usually in the same product category as the existing brand.

Brand Loyalty: active support by consumers in continuing sage/endorsement of one particular brand in the face of competition by other branded substitutes. The loyalty is often subjective or subconscious

Branding: creation of brand image through visual and verbal elements. Includes, but goes far beyond, 'brand name' and 'logo' alone.

Campaign: organized course of action, planned to achieve predetermined objectives. Can relate to any part of the promotional mix, i.e. advertising, sales promotion, public relations.

Canada: Computer Assisted New Drug Application. NDA submitted on CD-ROM and/or other electronic media.

Cannibalization: sales achieved for a particular brand at the expense of another brand within the same company.

Cash Cow: a well established product which is generating substantial revenue in excess of costs whilst retaining market share, i.e. high market share in a low growth market.

Competitive Strategy: the way in which a company chooses to compete within a market, with particular regard to the relative positioning and strategies of its competitors.

Consumer: 1. the ultimate user of a product, as opposed to the purchaser. 2. More generally, a person or household that uses or buys goods and services, as distinct from the producer and distributor.

Consumer Buying Behavior: buying behavior of ultimate consumers; persons who purchase products for personal or household use and not for business purposes.

Consumer Confusion Study: is a study that aims to measure the tendency of consumers to confuse the company that makes a particular brand with another company, or to confuse one brand with another.

Consumer Decision Making: the multi-stage decision process consumer's use in making purchases.

Consumer Education: structured teaching efforts to provide consumers with knowledge and skills to allocate their resources in the best way in the marketplace.

Circulation   (Appendix A)

Gross Circulation: All copies of print media that were printed and distributed either sold or complimentary.

Gross Paid Circulation: All copes of print media printed and sold.

Net Paid Circulation: All copies of print media sold less those return due to non-sell.

Penetration: Circulation within a certain area divided by total households within that same area, expressed as a percentage.

Macro Marketing: analysis of market/marketing processes from a broad perspective e.g. nation to investigate into economical, social, cultural and/or political perspectives

Ethical Products: products carrying brand names, which are not advertised to the public and supply can be regulated (e.g. prescription).

Market Demand: total volume of a specific product/service bought by a defined group of customers in a specific market area, in a specified time period.

Market Density: the number of potential customers within a unit of land area, such as a square mile.

Market Development: selling existing products into new segments or geographic markets.

Market Dynamics: the interaction of critical market factors on the behavior of products within that market, e.g. price, promotion, entry order, perceived product profile.

Market Evolution: market life cycles describing the "evolution" of a market/industry. (Stages: embryonic - growth – maturity - decline).

Market Leader: brand or product securing the greatest proportion of total sales within its field. May sometimes refer to the company marketing the brand or product concerned.

Marketing: the anticipation and identification of customer problems/needs, and the profitable meeting of these with information, products and services.

Readership/Reach/Coverage:

Readership: The number of different individuals with a certain area that read a print product with a given period of time.

Duplication: Number or percentage of people exposed to more than one media (e.g., reads multiple newspapers, magazines, television, radio, etc.

Impressions: are used primarily to calculate CPMs. Also used in sales presentations to demonstrate how impressive an and campaign will be

Reader Profile or Composition:

Composition: Demographic profile of an audience

GRP s: 1.0 GRP, 1% of the specified target population in a particular area (also called a "rating") Adults 18+

Reader/Viewer Profile: The demographic characteristics of people exposed to a media schedule.

TRPs : 1% of the specified target population in a particular area (also called a "rating") Adults HHI $75K+ and college grads+

GRPs/TRPs: are a means to measure and compare the impact of different media buys:

- Newspaper alone

- Newspaper with radio

- Newspaper with TV and Radio

- TV Alone

- Radio Alone

Media: (See Appendix B:)

CPM: Cost to reach 1,000 people (unit cost divided by circulation multiplied by 1,000.

Average Frequency: Number of times individuals are exposed to an advertising message.

Frequency Distribution: A means to measure and compare the effectiveness of different med buys; Greatest reach at agreeable frequency levels; Judgement based on many factors: targets, product, creative, etc.

GRP: (Gross Rating Points) The sum of ratings delivered by a given list of media vehicles. The total of percent reached multiplied by the frequency.

Index: A ration (most times expressed in percentage) that relates numbers to a base. A par index equals 100 where the expected audience is equal to the base.

Georgraphic:

DMA: Designated Market Area (an area defined by A.C. Nielsen that relates to broadcast coverage; typically used for readership.

NDM: Newspaper Designated Market (an area defined by each Newspaper that relates to their primary market area; typically used for circulation).

Tabulation: is a frequency count of each question's answers.

Tachistoscope: is a device that allows a participant to look at some stimulus material (e.g. packaging or a brand name) for a pre-defined brief period of time. The aim is to investigate the stand out and/or recognisability of the material under investigation.

Tactics: the detailed components of a strategy contained within a marketing plan explaining in detail what actions are to be taken to meet the objectives set.

Target Audience: see Target Market.

Target Market: a segment of the market or group of people, which has been selected as a focus for the company's offering or communications.

1.7 Overview of the Study

A. Advertising Outlook

Research on human motivation, used a pyramid to show our "hierarch of needs." De Joseph, Adweek, 2003). Each building block supports the next level.

The blocks at the bottom represent our most primitive needs: to eat, to have a roof over ones head, to have a feeling of safety and security. As these basics are taken care of, we turn to social needs – the need to belong to a group. Then comes the ego level, or esteem: the need to gain approval. At the top of the pyramid is self-actualization, the ability to realize one's potential.

Over the last five decades, society has mirrored the Maslow pyramid that has been reflected in our advertising and marketing approaches. In the 50' and early '60's, the Cold War brought with it the need to feel safe and secure. People built fallout shelters in their backyards. Dad worked for the same company his whole life. Mom stayed home and served the kids a nice warm bowl of Campbell's soup, some Poppin' Fresh Pillsbury muffins or a tasty piece of Betty Crocker cake. From the late '60s to the early 70's, the importance of the group took over. There was in increase in social action, protest marches, feminism. Belonging was a basic need. Charlie Tuna was always trying to picket Starkist.

Ego and esteem, the next level in the pyramid, were popular in the '70s and 80's – "The Me Decade" emerged. Social consciousness took a back seat to individual achievement and empower. The "singles scene" erupted, as did AIDS. The '80s saw the emergence of the "personal" computer. In the late '80s and '90s, we arrived at the top of the pyramid – self-actualization. The human body became an art form to be sculpted, tattooed and fed antioxidants. We cocooned and personalized our entertainment by surfing the Net and the cable stations. Even the TV idols were self-involved types – *Seinfeld* and *Friends*. The '90s officially ended on September 11, 2001. Now, with terrorism, corporate corruption and recession, we've slid down the pyramid and back to our quest for security, safety and stability. Corporations as well as individuals are evaluating their priorities. Risk-taking, once seen as a component of corporate success, has been replaced by corporate honesty and integrity.

Society will never go back to the days of Ozzie and Harriet. But, knowing this, how can businesses and smart advertisers interpret society's clear and present need for a sense of security in their messages? They might start by being truthful and straight with the consumers. Security should be at the core of their messaging. Consumers today have little tolerance for hype. "Be all you can be" wouldn't work today, nor would "Greed is good."

Advertisers who stress brand qualities like dependability, consistency and customer service will have the advantage. This is a particularly good time for "challenger" brands to make their move, simply because they carry no baggage from past messaging. It is also an opportunity to keep the message consistent across all platforms. Consistency translates to trust and comfort.

B. The Business of Advertising is Under Pressure

Digital technologies, shifting consumer behavior and demands accountability threaten in some cases already damaged decade-old business models. As the industry confronts change, it is increasingly clear that the tools and key metrics used as the basis for hundreds of billions of dollars spent on media, especially TV and print, may no longer be adequate to the task. As flaws and inefficiencies become more visible in media currencies such as the Nielsen ratings, the industry faces major hurdles in turning dissatisfaction into action to shift the market to more accurate and relevant tools. That reflects the enormity of the challenge as well as a deep-seated resistance to change – a painful, messy process without a clear outcome.

C. Newspaper Print Media's Declining Circulation

Publishers Fret about circulation declines especially the decline in Sunday readership. For better or for worse, it's the heart of the product, supplying an estimated 40% of the industry's advertising lifeblood. But circulation volume has been flagging faster on Sunday than on weekdays for several years. Demographic changes bode ill for papers in general;

they may hit Sunday editions especially hard. Lifestyle changes add to
the threat. The maturing of baby boomers has meant a great portion of
Americans working longer workweeks over the past quarter-century,
meaning they have to cram more errands and chores into the weekend.
There's little time to relax, and more media sources are competing to fill it.
In order to compete with digital, cable, and the newer uses of various
technology currently used to capture consumer attention, both newspaper
and magazine has sacrificed integrity.   (Appendix C1)

D. Magazine Face Circulation Problems

Magazine circulation debates often come down to points of contention
about audit rules, rate bases and selling subscriptions cheap. Advertisers
run ads to reach customers, so advertisers should be interested in those
magazines that can most efficiently reach the desired audience.
Publishers should focus on the value of the product to the advertisers and
the readers. Manipulating numbers to disclose reach to the audit bureaus
supercedes any other accountability. (Appendix B7)

E. Interactive Advertising (Appendix A & B)

F.   Television Vision/Cable Advertising   (Appendix B, B2, B4),

G. Point-of-Purchase Value (Appendix B3)

In-store advertising has seen growth of investment in retail outlets and more experimentation in recent years, but advertisers and agencies remain skeptical about the big question – Does it work?

Hitting consumers with media advertising in the store, where Point-of-Purchase Advertising International says 74% of all buying decisions are made, is disarmingly sensible, say even the most harden in-store skeptics. Marketers say it doesn't help the credibility of new in-store media when they're often sold in an age-old way – through arm-twisting by retail buyers whose chains sometimes view these media more as a profit center than a way to move merchandise. There is a lot of testing and experimenting going on (with in store advertising).

2a. <u>The Basics For Women</u>

Many of the conditions associated with an increased risk of cardiovascular diseases affect both genders. These risk facts include high blood pressure, high blood cholesterol, obesity, tobacco smoke, physical inactivity and diabetes. Whether you're a man or a woman, if you keep your blood pressure and cholesterol under control, maintain a healthy weight, don't smoke, eat a healthy diet and engage in regular physical activity, you'll reduce your personal odds of having a heart attack or stroke.   Woman have additional considerations to take into account, Low HDL ("good") cholesterol or diabetes takes an even greater toll on a woman's heart than a man's (Goldberg, MD 2003).

Ideally a woman begins to take steps to prevent heart disease in her twenties. Starting off by following up on family history of hear disease, high blood pressure or high cholesterol. As you increase in age and the risk increases because of blood pressure, cholesterol begins to rise and weight gain tends to increase, all factors that increase the risk of heart disease. This is the time to be proactive with your health regimen.

2b. Basics for Men

The journey to a healthy heart starts with the first step – talking to ones physician. Discuss nutrition, alcohol use, and physical activity. Chart your blood pressure, weight, blood cholesterol, glucose levels, etc. Armed with this information doctors can provide a "global risk assessment" that will tell you your chances of developing heart diseases over the course of a decade.

2c. Basics for Children (Surgeon Generals Report)

- In 2000, 13% of children aged 6 to 11 years and 14% of adolescents aged 12 to 19 years in the United States were overweight. This prevalence has nearly tripled for adolescents in the past 2 decades.

- Risk factors for heart disease, such as high cholesterol and high blood pressure, occur with increased frequency in overweight children and adolescents compared to children with a healthy weight.

- Type 2 diabetes, previously considered an adult disease, has increased dramatically in children and adolescents. Overweight and obesity are closely linked to type 2 diabetes.

- Overweight adolescents have a 70% chance of becoming overweight or obese adults. This increases to 80% if one or more

- parent is overweight or obese. Overweight or obese adults are at risk for a number of health problems including heart disease, type 2 diabetes, high blood pressure, and some forms of cancer.

- The most immediate consequence of overweight as perceived by the children themselves is social discrimination. This is associated with poor self-esteem and depression

The Causes of Overweight

- Overweight in children and adolescents is generally caused by lack of physical activity, unhealthy eating patterns, or a combination of the two, with genetics and lifestyle both playing important roles in determining a child's weight.

- Our society has become very sedentary. Television, computer and video games contribute to children's inactive lifestyles.

- 43% of adolescents watch more than 2 hours of television each day.

- Children, especially girls, become less active as they move through adolescence.

3.1 Surgeon Generals Recommendation

- You don't need special skills or training to be physically active. Walking is a great way to be active.

- Physical activity should be initiated slowly, and the intensity should be increased gradually (e.g., start with a 10-minute walk three times a week and work your way up to 30 minutes of brisk walking or other form of moderate activity five times a week).

- Activities can be split into several short periods (e.g., 10 minutes 3 times a day) instead of one longer period (e.g., 30 minutes once a day).

- You should select activities that you **ENJOY** and can fit into your daily life.

- It may take time to incorporate more activity into your daily life. Don't get discouraged if at first you miss a day or two; just keep trying and do your best to make it a regular part of your life. You will soon realize how good it feels to be physically active and fit.

- Ask for support from friends and family; likewise, support the people in your life who are trying to be physically active.

- Many forms of physical activity can be social, allowing you to converse and spend time with family or friends or to develop new relationships.

- Make fitness a priority...**COMMIT TO IT**.

INTAKE	OUTPUT
Calories From Foods	Calories Used During Physical Activity

THE ENERGY BALANCE

* Consult with your health care provider before starting a vigorous exercise program if you have ever had heart trouble or high blood pressure or suffer from chest pains, dizziness or fainting, arthritis, or if you are over age 40 (men) or 50 (women).

- To maintain your weight, your intake of calories must equal your energy output.

- To lose weight, you must use more energy than you take in.

- A difference of one 12-oz. soda (150 calories) or 30 minutes of brisk walking most days can add or subtract approximately 10 pounds to your weight each year

3.2   TILT THE BALANCE WITH PHYSICAL ACTIVITY

- Adding moderate amounts of physical activity five or more times a week to your routine uses 150 calories of energy on each day of activity, which can be equivalent to approximately 5 pounds in 6 months or 10 pounds in 1 year.

- You can choose any combination of type of activity at the length of time specified from the following table to burn approximately 150 calories:

- Reducing your calorie intake by 150 calories a day, along with participating in moderate activity, could double your weight loss and is equivalent to approximately 10 pounds in 6 months and 20 pounds in 1 year.

4. The Captivating Media Frinzy

"Paging Dr. Fatkins?" In the low-carb vs. low-fat war the media has

turned intelligent, conscientious people into confused, irrational individuals

who jump on any product or miracle devise that will make them happy and

health in 30-days, guaranteed.

The fast food industry is getting hit the hardest and has dug in their

heels to survive by trying to adjust to the consumers' demands. Some

realistic, many are not.

4a. Donut Makers Must Fry, Fry Again

Headlines: A 68-year old health food executive is serving 15 months in a federal prison. His crime: willfully mislabeling doughnuts as low fat. The label read three grams of fat and 135 calories. Analysis from the Food and Drug Administration showed that the doughnut, glazed with chocolate contained 18 grams of fat and 530 calories. The FDA responded that if it sounds to good to be true, it probably is. (Shirlye Leung, Wall Street Journal, January 2004)

4b. No Super Size For You

Under fire for its menu amid obesity concerns McDonald's Corporation decided as of January, 2004 to phase out its trademark supersize fries and drinks in the U.S. McDonalds was one of the primary chains that popularized giant-size fast food meals over a decade ago. The company is now trying to streamline its core menu emphasizing a balanced diet.

This decision also falls on the heels of the new consumer wave of frivolous lawsuits filed towards eateries that allowed them to eat their way to obesity. Many citing that it was not their desire to super-size but the pressure felt with the counter server used the "will that be super-sized" phrase to up-sell coupled with the low cost difference making one fill momentarily inadequate for not accepting an offer that gives you one-third more for only pennies.

4c.   Fast Food's Position on Obesity

For years, Colonel Harland Sanders carried the secret formula for his Kentucky Fried Chicken in his head and the spice mixture in his car. Today, the recipe is locked away in a safe in Louisville, Ky. Only a handful of people know that multi-million dollar recipe for the deep fried in minutes in a pressure cooker technique that made finger licking and art. As consumers started focusing on healthier eating in the late '80's a marketing strategy made the deep fried delight healthier by taking the word "fried" out of it's name. Branding the fast food establishment as "KFC" without changing the grease content in the food preparation apparently made this delicacy a healthier choice.

KFC's attempt in the millennium to position it's self as a healthy choice was a short –term promotional disaster. The nation's obesity numbers are growing, the new Taco Bell is pacing with the big boys, but selling fried chicken, as part of a healthy diet was a preposterous strategy. (Barbara Lippert, Adweek, 2003)

Nutritionists warn dieter the current mania for low-carbohydrates, high protein foods-fueled by Atkins and South Beach diets is unhealthy and possibly dangerous. Pushing weight-sensitive Americans away from whole grains and towards saturated fats, bread is unappetizing to dieters.

It's quite a comedown for bread, long touted as an essential element in the U.S. Food and Drug Administration's food pyramid. (H.Lee Murphy) Crains, Jan. 2004.

4D.　　Targeting the Youth Market

Trends live fast and die young. Thanks to teens' enormous and growing consumer power – They spent $175 billion dollars in 2003. The age group is more than enticing. Teens are trend-obsessed – yet their preoccupation with the "next big thing" can be a double –edge sword. (Zollo, Crains 2004).

Young people are particularly receptive to messages that promise either a new experience or one that satisfies a need that is unique to this group. But they're also adept at blocking out messages they deem false or misdirected. Brands that over promise, under-deliver or falter even slightly in an ads tone or execution is often shocked to learn just how unforgiving teens can be.

Example, a couple of years ago the term "extreme" gained popularity as a way to describe action sports that favored high adrenaline and independence over teamwork and tradition. Marketers seized the moment and began to capitalize on "extreme" lifestyles to convey their brands as youthful, daring and rebellious. The imagery was a natural fit for athletic-related brands, the lifestyle's focus on fitness and activity made high-calorie snack foods and soft drinks less appropriate choices. Still these products promised increased energy or a "flavor rush" that teens accepted.

Later the shampoo and toothpaste industries tried to take advantage of this gravy train – by then teens concluded that these products had not only showed up late to the party, but, the train had already left the station.   Late entry into a youth craze can damage brand credibility.

As marketers become more youth-savvy, they keep a trained eye on emerging trends. This attention often results in an abbreviated life cycle for many trends. Typically, there is a group of teens that standout from the rest, they are the trendsetters. They value you the attention they get from being at the top of the hierarchy. These are the people marketer must keep an eye on. As products become mainstream, this trend setting group begins to abandon the trend which starts a negative ripple effect that can find a product lingering on the shelf as the trend setters are

awaiting the next new thing with their followers in tow.

5a. <u>Coke Sets its Sights on Teens</u>

Soft drink giant aims to cultivate youthful image by marketing a chill out

zone in the local malls. Coca-Cola Company wants to convince teens that

shopping goes better with Coke. The beverage giant opened a branded chill-

out environment called "Coca-Cola Read Lounge" with shopping center

partner Westfield Corporation in the December of 2003. A place for the under

20-year-old mall rat. The premier lounges opened in Los Angeles and a

Chicago suburb. Coke hopes to convince teens that it's hip and young – co-

opting an image rival PepsiCo. Has owned for years. (MacArthur, 2003)

5b.   <u>Pepsi Acknowledges Point of Cola Advertising</u>

One of the great mysteries of the modern world – Why, in the face

of such compelling reasons to drink Coke and Pepsi, have both

companies spent billions of dollars over the past 20 years showing

impossibly attractive young people having lifestyle moments with sugar

water? The latest meaningless theme "it's the cola". It's a fine

complement to tortilla chips, wing-dings, and hotdogs – a geared toward

the youth market. (Garfield, 2003).   Selecting spokes people to reach the youth group such as African-American comedian, Bernie Chappell and new reality television idol, 20-year old Paris Hilton.

5c.   Cell Phones Attack the Youth Market

Cell phones change their look to reach the teen seen. Colorful interchangeable face places, ear buds, flashing lights and sleeker to fit in the pocket of those jeans.

Time Warner's Broadcasting System introduced during Christmas of 2003 Cartoon Network characters such as Tom and Jerry, The Flintstones, and the Power Puff Girls on wireless products. By the beginning of 2004 mobile users will be able to pit Tom in ballets against Jerry, personalize handsets with picture messages and screen savers. Send friends animated pictures. Users can preview and purchase icons at a Cartoon Network's wireless website, paying per download or by monthly fee. (Wentz, 2003).

5d. Beer Makers Target Youths

Anheuser-Busch Co. has been accused of targeting the youth market . The beer manufacturer has partnered with many events that are targeted towards youth awareness. Their soft marketing approach is raising brand awareness before these young adults reach legal drinking age.   By sponsoring high school and college sporting events. Their logos wave high above stadiums across the country.

In an aggressive move that started in the late 1990's, the spirits industry has partnered with companies such as "Student Travels". These companies plan 7-10 vacations for graduating high school students to take class trips after graduation to places such as the Caribbean. Islands were the drinking age is supposedly 18, with no-one policing the beaches and bikini clad models handing out free beer and wine with someone in a beer bottle custom clowning about on the beaches attracting the kids to try the their ice cold brews – the message is more aggressive and branding is key. For over a period of 7 to 14 days these kids are frolicking the beaches enjoying all the free alcohol the can guzzle before passing out. In the past years these excursions have become fatal to at least one or two of these teens whose trip home has been in a body bag.

Teinowitz (2003) Superior Court in the District of Columbia bought a suit charging that alcohol marketers engage "in active, deliberate and concerted efforts to maximize their profits by attempting to establish brand loyalty among underage consumers". The suit alleges alcohol marketers, using code words and denials to cover their real marketing intentions, using cartoon characters, video game references and other devices in ads

running on youth-oriented media to violate industry ad codes of
acceptability.

CHAPTER 2

REVIEW OF RELATED LITERATURE

2.1.1 <u>Marketing and Morality</u>

Consideration of the moral dimension of marketing has increased
significantly in recent years. Areas of literature such as marketing ethics
and green marketing have experienced rapid development since their
emergence in the 1980's. New forms of behavior such as ethical
consumerism and ethical branding have opened up entirely new areas of
literature.

1. Macromarketing

2. Social Marketing

3. Societal marketing

There is evidence of moral issues entering marketing disciplines
consideration of morality.   Robin and Reidenback (1993) have shown that
there are two broad areas in which moral questions can arise marketing.

1. Macromarketing questions, which relate to the morality of marketing
as a discipline, function or process in it.

2.   Narrower Macromarketing questions, which questions morality in relation to the specific actions of individuals, marketers, marketing organizations and marketing industries.

The moral basis of marketing theory is based upon the notion of the sovereign consumer, and it is perhaps unsurprising that both marketing theory and practice are replete with the discourse of consumer sovereignty. (Dixon 1992, Knights etc al. 1994; Christensen 1995). Most common definitions of marketing and the marketing concept tend to be predicated on the consumer sovereignty model, with emphasis firmly placed on the need for "customer orientation", "customer focus", "customer-driven strategies", or some such version of what is essential and "outside-in perspective". The following, taken from one popular text book (Kotler et al.   1996), is indicative of most definitions of marketing concepts, and is explicit in its promotion of Galbraith's (1972) accepted sequence:

The marketing concept holds that achieving organizational goals depends on determining the needs and wants of target markets and delivering the desired satisfactions more effectively and efficiently than competitors do. (Kotler et al. 1996: 15).

The discourse of consumer sovereignty has by now permeated beyond marketing into a broad range of theoretical and practical arenas of management in contemporary organizations and organizational theory (Du Gay and Salaman 1992). It is however, based on two critical assumptions: (i) that needs originate from the consumer; and (ii) that firms identify and act upon these needs when translated into consumer demand (Galbraith 1972); Dixon 1992; Knights et al. 1994). As we shall see, both of these have been criticized as empirically inaccurate.

Knights et al. (1994) have analyzed the financial services market to illustrate how profit and cost concerns can channel as well as limit the attention accorded to consumer need. Moreover, they argue that consumer indifference can prompt firms to create rather than follow demand, such as through 'informing and 'educating' customers of new technologies, beliefs and ways of behaving. Indeed, the creation of new markets that do not yet exist, and of going beyond what the customer thinks s/he wants, is being increasingly touted as the pre-eminent marketing strategy of successful, forward-thinking companies. (Hamel and Prahalad 199, 1994; Martin 1995).

2.1.2   Impact of Marketing on Society

Even if it could be argued that the consumer was fully sovereign in the
economy, this would not necessarily provide a moral justification for
traditional marketing theory. The concept is concerned with marrying
individual customer satisfaction with firm profitability. As Dixon (1992)
argues though, this does not necessarily mean that social good is
maximized. The consumption decision is an inherently individual one,
where we seek to satisfy our own immediate needs and desires. For the
most part, social concerns are not a significant force in our consumption
decisions, since these are essentially about long-term, shared aspects of
our lives. We might then distinguish between our concerns as consumers
(what we want for ourselves) and our concerns as citizens (what we want
for everyone); we are as Sagoff (1986) put it, essentially schizophrenic.
The justification for ethical consumerism and green marketing. This then is
an extraordinarily rich vein of research, but as Desmond (1998) notes, this
plurality of approaches represents a fragmented response, and might
more accurately be discussed in terms of 'marketing' rather than a unified
academic literature. However, each of these trends makes an important
contribution to our understanding of marketing and morality, and
throughout these readings we'll draw on all of these in order to provide
deeper understanding of this area.

2.1.3   Green Marketing and Morality

The main aim of the empirical study reported here was to analyze whether, and in which ways, morality was given or denied meaning and expression in green marketing practices. The three organizations context – conventional, social mission and business-NGO collaboration respectively – as well as setting out the cultural dynamics through which moral meanings are identified. Various elements pertaining to the moral dimension of these processes and dynamics have been identified, leading to some preliminary construction of theoretical categories, constructs and propositions regarding moral meaning in marketing. (Crane, Andrew) 2001).

2.1.4   Ethics & Manipulation in Advertising

This book critically analyzes an attack on advertising that has been a permanent feature of American intellectual life since at least the 1930s. Briefly put, the attack says that advertising manipulates consumers, and that this manipulation justifies corrective political action. This attack's influence waxes and wanes, but it is never without adherents. It finds support because it is initially plausible, and because many people find its political conclusions congenial. By and large, however, there is little to support this assault on advertising. Advertising almost certainly does not manipulate as well as its critics believe. (Phillips, Michael J. 1997).

This book undermines a critique of advertising that emphasizes its manipulativeness. Phillips, agenda ranges from modest recommendations for increased regulation of certain ads, through proposals to limit the volume of advertising, to John Kenneth Galbraith's ambitious program for less consumerist America. After developing this book's conception of the term "manipulative advertising," the chapters observe that because advertising's manipulativeness might be a good thing – by hypothesis it keeps the economy humming, after all – its critics badly need a moral argument to justify their political agenda. That agenda is a complete non sequitur even if advertising's powers are enormous. Advertising's traditional critics, many of whom were economists and implicit utilitarian, usually were not too articulate about the moral underpinnings of their works. But with the emergence of the business ethics movement in the 1970s and 1980s, moral arguments for manipulative advertising's badness finally became available.

2.2.1   <u>Overweight and Obesity: A Vision for the Future</u>

The nation must take an informed, sensitive approach to communicate with and educate the American people about health issues related to overweight and obesity. Everyone must work together to:

- Change the perception of overweight and obesity at all ages. Should be one of health and not appearance.

- Educate all expectant parents about the many benefits of breastfeeding.

- Educate health care providers and health profession students in the prevention and treatment of overweight and obesity across the lifespan.

- Provide culturally appropriate education in schools and communities about healthy eating habits and regular physical activity, based on the Dietary Guidelines for American's for people of all ages. Emphasize the consumer's role in making wise food and physical activity choices.

The nation must take action to assist Americans in balancing healthful eating with regular physical activity. Individuals and groups across all settings must work in concert to:

- Ensure daily quality physical education in all school grades. Such education can develop the knowledge, attitudes, skills, behaviors and confidence needed to be physically active for life.

- Reduce time spent watching television and in other similar sedentary behaviors.

- Build physical activity into regular routines and playtime for children and their families, Ensure that adults get at least 30 minutes of moderate physical activity on most days of the week.

- Create more opportunities for physical activity at worksites. Encourage all employers to make facilities and opportunities available for physical activity for all employers.

- Promote healthier food choices, including at least 5 servings of fruits and vegetables each day, and reasonable portion sizes at home, in schools, at worksites, and in communities.

- Ensure that schools provide health foods and beverages on school campuses and at school events.

The nation must invest in research that improves our understanding of the causes, prevention and treatment over overweight and obesity. A concerted effort should be made. (Surgeon General Report, 2002).

2.2.2   Obesity Fight Starved For Cash

(Andrew Martin, 2004), The federal government is hoping to slow the obesity epidemic with a series of advertisements that suggest Americans can lose love handles and double chins by exercise more and eating healthier food.   But because the ads, unveiled in recent days, are public service announcements, the frequency with which Americans are reminded of the goals depends largely on the largest of television broadcasters and newspaper companies. Therein, some critics say, lies a key problem with the government's efforts to combat obesity and promote healthy eating, which   it has declared a top national priority. At a time when the beer industry spends more than $1 billion a year on advertising, the federal government is devoting relatively few dollars to promoting its nutrition campaign.

"This administration talks a lot about obesity and physical inactivity," said Margo Wootan, director of nutrition policy at the Center for Science in the Public Interest, a nutrition advocacy group in Washington. "But it's all talk and very little action. They're not putting money towards programs." While producers of candies, soft drinks, chips and other less-than-nutritious foods bombard consumers with thousands of prime-time ads, the Agriculture Department has budgeted $1.8 million to publicize its soon-to-be-released revised food pyramid. "the education campaign, whatever it is, goes up against $34 billion in food industry advertising a year", said Marion Nestle, a New York University nutritionist and a frequent critic of industry influence on government nutrition policies. "One million dollars or $2 million isn't even the ad budge for Altoids mints."

An analysis of advertising spending by the food industry shows just how much of   a climb the government faces in its battle to slim America's waistline. Conducted by TNS Media Intelligence/CMR, the analysis shows that some of the foods considered the least healthful advertise the most. Bear and ale advertising totaled $1.2 billion in 2002. More than $750 million was spent on soft-drink ads, $570 million on cereals and $545 million on candy and mints. During the same year, about $51 million was spent on advertising fruit and $47 million on vegetables.

John Webster, a spokesman for the Agriculture Department's Center for Nutrition Policy and Promotion that is revising the food pyramid, said the government doesn't just rely on advertising. In the case of the food pyramid, he said the USDA also counts on educators, government officials and nutritionists to disseminate its nutrition message.

2.2.3   Heavy Kids Menus

The Study by the Center for Science in the Public interest looks at children's menus at several popular restaurant chains, including

Applebee's, Chili's and Outback Steakhouse. Fried chicken fingers or

nuggets were found on each of the 20 kids' menus, and each one of the

menus featured fried potatoes as a side dish, the study found. Extras, like

complimentary sugar-laden desserts and sodas, added to the calorie

count. Although children may prefer burgers and chicken fingers, parent's

care about what their kids eat, and they need to have a choice.

(Dr. Michael Jacobson, 2004), "parents could simply skip the kids'

menu and get a healthy meal for themselves and split it with their kids."

Most of the children's meals contained somewhere between 600 and

1,000 calories, which is half a day's worth of the calories that children

ages 4 to 8 should be eating. "Limit or eliminate the amount of artery-

clogging "bad fat" (saturated plus trans-fat) to   17 grams, which is just

slightly less than the 20-gram "bad-fat" limit recommended for older

children and adults."

2.2.4   The Inactive Generation

(Mand, Adrienne, 2004), Most gyms cater to adult professionals,

people in their 20s and 30s. But one of the fastest-growing demographic

groups in the industry is people under 18. According to the international

Health, Racquet and Sports Club Association, this group's club

memberships grew 189 percent relative to the total number of members between 1987 and 200s.   There is a growing segment within the club industry that is committed to providing programming for the entire family," Siad Bill Howland, Director of research at IHRSCA. "The need for such services has never been more urgent," according to the Centers for Disease Control and Prevention; increasing numbers of children are obese or have high blood pressure or cholesterol levels.

2.3.1   Kneeling to Young Continues

(Moses, Lucia, 2003), The latest attempt to hook young readers took the shape of a free commuter paper. Many publishing executives are hard at work trying to launch publications tailored to reach 18-34 year olds. "Young readers don't seem interested in daily papers and definitely don't want to pay for content", said, Gary L. Watson, President of the California Newspaper Publishers Association.

Critics pounced on The Washington Posts' new Express, now the third commuter paper (others are in Boston and Philadelphia), calling it brief, bland, and lacking local news. Publisher Christopher Ma said the quick-read approach allows readers to catch up on the news and helps develop a daily reading habit among young people. The Chicago Tribune's RedEye is sticking to its plan to convert to paid, even though that has meant cutting distribution roughly in half since the fall 2002 launch.

2.3.2   <u>Sprite Shifts Gears</u>

"Coca-Cola company wants to make Sprite more relevant by adding some flava", statement released by WPP Group of Ogilvy & Mather, New York. In order to reach a young audience the new attitude will be personified in action figure "Miles Thirst" – a freethinking African-American poet/philosopher with a five-finger-high Afro and a hip-hop sensibility. PepsiCo's Sierra Mist has also poured on the pressure to expand its youth base. During the end of 2003 Coca-Cola began seeding the brand through DJs, sampling parties and events, sporting events, and a remix video shoot hosted by rapper, producer and music talent P.Diddy at the MTV Music Video awards. (MacArthur and Neff, 2004).

2.3.3   <u>RCN's New Cable Channel – Youth Target</u>

New York, Regional cable operator RCN Corp launched an alternative TV channel in seeks to interact with its audience, Viewers are invited to go on-line and critique the station's shows, and RCN is promising to drop programs they viewers don't like and will replace them with new ones. The Channel features a mixture of syndicated and original programs, including short films, music videos, fitness shows, and cartoons

2.3.4   Volvo Goes After Younger Buyers

The marketers is hoping to build on its current sales tear, is looking to lure twenty-something buyers by tying in the Microsoft's Xbox and Virgin Group. It's creating commercials with hip-hop band Dilated Peoples and music video directory Dave Myers. (Halliday, Jean, 2004).   "It's unusual to say Volvo and hot in the same sentence, said Wes Brown, an analyst at Car Consultant Iceology, but it is important to secure a younger market for high-end luxury items."

CHAPTER 3

METHODOLOGY

3.1 Approach Effects of Marketing

Parsa and Lankford (1998) ethics may be defined as an "inquiry into the nature and grounds of morality where the term morality is taken to mean moral judgments, standards and rules of conduct." [Hunt and Vitell, 1988] Ethical theories in moral philosophy may be categorized as either deontological or teleological theories. Deontological theories deal mainly with the inherent righteousness of behavior. Teleological theories stress the amount of good or bad embodied in the consequence of the behaviors.

This research has opted to use a Teleological case approach to develop a model for the marketing industry because Advertising has different effects on consumers; it changes their prospective on what is, and what is not, worth buying, what they buy and when they buy it.   How advertisers target a certain background or area for their product, and how they get consumers attention to react positively or negatively.

3.2 Data Gathering Method

The case study method enables the researcher to review past and present observations and concepts found throughout the marketing teachings, advertising concept development and negative/positive outcomes. The selection of the study cases was chosen from marketing campaigns, and short-term and long-term effects in related marketing industry. These are current initiatives and are available on the Internet.

Statistics gathered from marketing research firms, advertising age and the U.S. Department of Healths' different websites.

3.3 Database of the Study

The database consists of the analysis of The Surgeon General (www.surgeongeneral.gov), New Dreams (www.newdream.org), Industry Leaders (www.economy.com). All are marketing and advertising major category resources.

The statistics database is from the American Heart Association

(www.americanheart.org that reviews heart healthy statistics and Adweek
(www.adweek.com) provides the most current ad campaigns and reports
statistics on consumer reaction.

3.4 Validity of the Data

The media industry understands the importance of accountability
research that assesses ROI. In the last two years, two recognized experts
in this field – Marketing Management Analytics and the Hudson River
Group – were commissioned to perform "hands-off" multi-media analyses
to determine medias' role in contributing to advertising ROI; role of
audience measurement as part of media planning and buying and the
review of short-term and long-term results of consumer behavior. The
study cases are valid to project and to propose the process and to define
what the key drivers are in the advertising industry.

3.4.1 Validity of Teen of Teen Data

Because a primary objective of The TRU (Teenage Research
Unlimited) Study is to track market changes and trends, it is essential that
methodology be approached systematically. From sample design and data
collection to data editing and weighting, each detail uniformly conforms to
predetermined specifications. Only through such an approach can data

purity be assured and market changes and trends be reliably uncovered.

Sample Design

To achieve the greatest sampling precision, TRU utilizes a stratified sample design. The following factors are multiplied to create 144 demographic clusters (strata), from which the sample is based (2S x 8A x 9G = 144):

- Sex (Approximately 51% male; 49% female.)

- Age (Distribution of 12-19 year olds proportionate to U.S. Census data ranging from 11.6% to 13.1% for a single age group.)

- Geography (In proportion to actual teen population distribution among the nine Census divisions.)

Names are selected on an Nth basis within each of the 144 clusters. A fresh sample is constructed for each six-month wave.

Sampling Procedure

A self-executing mail survey is used to collect the data. The survey instrument is a colorful, digest-size questionnaire booklet. The questionnaire is mailed directly to the teen names selected. The sampling procedure is executed in four phases; a pre-alert postcard, the mailing of the survey package (which includes a unique interactive peel-off sticker for added incentive), and a telephone follow-up with second mailing.

Pre-Alert Postcard: Mailed to the sample approximately 10 days before the arrival of the survey package, the pre-alert informs teens of their selection as "survey members" and advises them to watch the mail for the soon-to-arrive survey package.

The **Survey Package** includes:

- A hand-stamped outer envelope

- A cover letter

- A questionnaire booklet

- A one-dollar bill

- A colorful peel-off sticker (which respondents remove from the letter and place on the questionnaire's front page, signaling TRU's remitting to them an additional five dollars).

- A postage-paid reply envelope.

Telephone Contact/Follow-up Mailing: Approximately three to four weeks after the original mailing, non-respondents are contacted by telephone. Those who still have their survey package are encouraged to return their completed survey questionnaire. Those who have misplaced their original questionnaire are sent a second survey package.

Qualitative Pre- and Post-Research

Before each new study, TRU conducts a series of focus groups both among its Trendwatch panelists (mostly for investigation of new areas/questions and to test the questionnaire's overall timeliness) and an ad-hoc sample of teens from the youngest end of the target (to assure that new questions in development are easily understood). Once TRU receives back initial study data, analytic post focus groups among Trendwatch panelists are conducted to obtain teens' unique insights into the findings. Some of the verbatims from these groups are also interspersed throughout the report (under the title of "Teen Talk") to add a further qualitative dimension to the data.

Statistical Balancing and Weighting

Though the mailing sample is in proportion to actual population distribution according to the most current U.S. Census data by age, sex, and region, the returned, usable questionnaires do not match as precisely. To achieve compatibility, then, with actual teen population distribution, balancing factors are applied to 64 demographic clusters, achieved by multiplying sex, age, and four (African American, Hispanic, White, and Other) race/ethnic groups (2S x 8A x 4R = 64). The result of this type of sample balancing procedure, known as successive approximation, is that the final in-tab sample is in exact proportion to the current U.S. teenage population in terms of sex, age, and race. It is also extremely close in terms of region (without the benefit of balancing), averaging a difference of less than one percent from Census data.

In addition to balancing the sample, weights are applied using the same algorithm to each of the same 64 demographic clusters to project the data to the national teenage population.

3.5 Limitations of the Study

The most important limitation of the study is that the topic of ethics in advertising marketing is an age old concern that has been addressed for well over fifty years and to date has no definitive conclusion. Every generation approaches this topic with a preconceived agenda that is not necessarily directed to the greater good of mankind.

Another limitation is the abundance of topical resources that appear to be valid references. Special interest groups and independent consultants soliciting their research to the highest bidder commission much of these readings. This can taint the outcome of the research.

The researcher has a background in developing advertising marketing campaigns across various media, has performed these day-to-day duties imposing ones own ethical agenda, but has not always been supported by the masses trying to create a bottom line.

The overall study is divided into three parts: Ethics in marketing and advertising literature, the effects of marketing directed at two major money making markets and the overhaul of various advertising campaigns due to FCC regulations. Business people sometimes praise advertising because it keeps the economy growing. Thus, if the theory is valid, utility is the sole criterion for determining the rightness or wrongness of manipulative advertising.

CHAPTER 4

DATA ANALYSIS

4.1 Obesity Identified

Obesity is the excessive accumulation of adipose tissue to an extent

that health is impaired.(1) Obesity is usually determined using the body

mass index or BMI. The National Heart, Lung, and Blood Institute (NHLBI)

Obesity Education Initiative Expert Panel developed guidelines for

identification, assessment and treatment of obesity. (2) The Practical

Guide: Identification Evaluation and Treatment of Overweight and Obesity

in Adults)

Overweight and obesity has reached epidemic proportions in the

United States, as well as worldwide.(3) Data collected by the National

Center for Health Statistics indicate that the prevalence of obesity, defined

as a body mass index >30 kg/m² has increased from 12.8% in 1976-1980

to 22.5% in 1988-1994 and 30% in 1999-2000. 4) Roughly 31% of

American adults meet the criterion for obesity - about 59 million American

adults. More than 64% of the US adult population have a BMI >=25

kg/m².(4) In an effort to increase public awareness of the epidemic

proportion of obesity, the Surgeon General has issued a call to action to

prevent and treat overweight and obesity and their associated health
complications.

4.1.1 Obesity and Diabetes

Over seventeen million Americans (6.2% of the population) have
diabetes. Almost 6 million Americans are unaware they have the
disease. There are two main types of diabetes. Both types are caused
by problems in how a hormone called insulin (that helps regulate blood
sugar) works. Type 1 diabetes most often appears in childhood or
adolescence and causes high blood sugar when your body can't make
enough insulin. Over 90% of all diabetes cases are what we call type 2
diabetes. Type 2 diabetes is usually diagnosed after age forty; however
it is now being found in all ages including children and adolescents.
Type 2 diabetes is linked to obesity and physical inactivity. In this form of
diabetes your body makes insulin but can't use its insulin properly. At
first, your body overproduces insulin to keep blood sugar normal, but
over time this causes your body to lose its ability to produce enough
insulin to keep blood sugar levels in the normal healthy range. The result
is sugar rises in your blood to high levels. Over a long period of time,
high blood sugar levels and diabetes can cause heart disease, stroke,
blindness, kidney failure, leg and foot amputations, and pregnancy

complications. Diabetes can be a deadly disease: over 200,000 people die each year of diabetes related complications.

How does weight relate to type 2 diabetes?

Carrying extra body weight and body fat go hand and hand with the development of type 2 diabetes. People who are overweight are at much greater risk of developing type 2 diabetes than normal weight individuals. Being overweight puts added pressure on the body's ability to properly control blood sugar using insulin and therefore makes it much more likely for you to develop diabetes. Almost 90% of people with type 2 diabetes are overweight. The number of diabetes cases among American adults jumped by a third during the 1990s, and more increases are expected. This rapid increase in diabetes is due to the growing prevalence of obesity and extra weight in the United States population.

What can one do to prevent diabetes?

The good news is type 2 diabetes is largely preventable. Research studies have found that lifestyle changes and small amounts of weight loss in the range of 5-10% can prevent or delay the development of type 2 diabetes among high-risk adults. Lifestyle interventions including diet and moderate-intensity physical activity (such as walking for 150 minutes per week) were used in these research studies to produce small amounts of weight loss. The development of diabetes was reduced 40% to 60% during these studies that lasted 3 to 6 years. Preventing weight gain, increasing activity levels and working toward small amounts of weight loss if you are overweight can have a big impact on the likelihood that you will develop diabetes in the future. Managing your weight is the best thing you can do to prevent the development of diabetes.

What can you do if you already have diabetes?

You can have a positive influence on your blood sugar and your overall health by choosing foods wisely, exercising regularly, reducing your stress level, and making modest lifestyle changes. Small amounts of weight loss (losing 10 pounds or more) can also have a big effect on how easily you can keep your blood sugar in the healthy range and can help prevent the complication of diabetes. Small amounts of weight reduction can decrease the amount of medication you need to keep your blood sugar in the healthy range. Overall better nutrition, physical activity, and control of blood glucose levels can delay the progression of diabetes and prevent complications.

4.1.2   Obesity and Cancer

Evidence for a link between cancer and obesity and overweight:

Considerable evidence suggests that obesity and overweight play an important role in cancer. Obesity and overweight have been clearly associated with increased risks for kidney cancer in both men and women (two-fold increased relative risk), and in women, endometrial cancer (one and a half-fold relative risk) and postmenopausal breast cancer (two-fold relative risk). Building evidence suggests that obesity and overweight also are associated with an increase risk of colorectal cancer, gall bladder cancer, and perhaps more modestly, the risk of thyroid cancer in women. For colorectal cancer, the effect of obesity and overweight on risk may be due in part to low physical activity, as consistent evidence exists for a strong protective effect of physical activity against developing colorectal cancer. Recent studies suggest that obesity and overweight may also play a role in the increasing incidence of some types of esophageal cancer, possibly through obesity's association with gastric reflux. For prostate cancer risk, inconsistent findings from studies evaluating obesity may result from

limitations in the measurement of obesity, as more consistent results
have come from recent studies of biological factors that are more
directly associated with specific aspects of body composition (e.g., total
fat).

For other types of cancer, in general, too few studies have been
conducted to draw conclusions about the relationship between obesity
and risk of disease development. However, strong experimental
research in animal models of cancer development and disease
progression have shown that maintenance of adequate and not
overweight body size can delay development of cancer. Whether this
can be achieved in humans has not been evaluated in prospective
randomized trials.

Cancers with lower rates among obese:

Obesity may also be somewhat protective against other forms of
cancer. Among premenopausal women, heavier women appear to
experience modest protection from breast cancer compared to leaner
women (0.7-fold relative risk). Lung cancer is also less prevalent among
the obese relative to leaner individuals (relative risk 0.7), possibly
because of smoking-related effects on metabolism, although some

investigators have argued that smoking or weight loss due to undetected disease may bias reported findings.

Cancer Death Rates and Obesity:

Evaluating the influence of obesity on survival from cancer is complicated by a number of factors including variation in treatment regimens and completeness of vital status follow-up. For most types of cancer, little data exists on this topic, except for breast cancer. Most studies of obesity and breast cancer survival, but not all, suggest that obese women have poorer survival than leaner women. To date, little is know about the mechanisms that might contribute to this effect and no prospective randomized trials have been conducted.

Trends in cancer related to obesity:

Like obesity, cancer is a major health problem in the United States and in other countries as well. Based on the American Cancer Society's 2002 estimates for cancer incidence, cancers linked to obesity among women comprise approximately 51% of all new cancers diagnosed among women in 2002: 2% thyroid cancers (15,800 new cases), 6% uterine cancers (39,300 new cases), 12% colorectal cancers (75,700 new cases), and 31% breast cancers (203,500 new cases). Among men, cancers linked to obesity comprise approximately 14% of new cancers: 3% kidney cancers (19,100 new cases) and 11% colorectal cancers (72,600 new cases). In terms of mortality, for women, obesity-related cancers are estimated to comprise 28% of cancer-related deaths in 2002: 15% breast cancers (39,600 deaths), 2% uterine cancers (6,600 deaths), and 11% colorectal cancers (28,800 deaths). Among men, obesity-related cancers are estimated to comprise 13% of cancer-related deaths in 2002: 10% colorectal cancers (27,800 deaths) and 3% kidney cancers (7,200 deaths).

Overall, while the mechanisms underlying the obesity-carcinogenesis relationship are not fully understood, sufficient evidence exists to support recommendations that adults and children maintain reasonable weight for their height and ages for multiple health benefits, including decreasing their risk of cancer. (NASO Study, 2004).

4.1.3   Obesity from Childhood:

Prevalence

In the past 30 years, the occurrence of overweight in children has doubled and it is now estimated that one in five children in the US is overweight. Increases in the prevalence of overweight are also being seen in younger children, including preschoolers. Prevalence of overweight is especially higher among certain populations such as

Hispanic, African American and Native Americans where some studies

indicate prevalence of >85th percentile of 35-40%. Also, while more

children are becoming overweight, the heaviest children are getting even

heavier. As a result, childhood overweight is regarded as the most

common prevalent nutritional disorder of US children and adolescents,

and one of the most common problems seen by pediatricians.

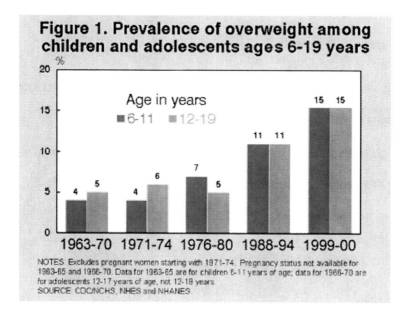

Figure 1. Prevalence of overweight among children and adolescents ages 6-19 years

NOTES: Excludes pregnant women starting with 1971-74. Pregnancy status not available for 1963-65 and 1966-70. Data for 1963-65 are for children 6-11 years of age; data for 1966-70 are for adolescents 12-17 years of age, not 12-19 years.
SOURCE: CDC/NCHS, NHES and NHANES.

Consequences of Childhood Overweight

Both the short term and long term effects of overweight on health are of

concern because of the negative psychological and health

consequences in childhood.

Potential Negative Psychological Outcomes:

- Depressive symptoms

- Poor Body Image

- Low Self-Concept

- Risk for Eating Disorders

- Negative Health Consequences:

- Insulin Resistance

- Type 2 Diabetes

- Hypertension

- High Total and LDL Cholesterol and triglyceride levels in the blood

- Low HDL Cholesterol levels in the blood

- Sleep Apnea

- Early puberty

- Orthopedic problems such as Blount's disease and slipped capital femoral epiphysis

- Non-alcoholic steatohepatitis (fatty infiltration and inflammation of the liver)

Further, obese children are more likely to be obese as adults, hence they are at increased risk for a number of diseases including: stroke, cardiovascular disease, hypertension, diabetes, and some cancers

Contributors to Childhood Overweight

- Food Choices - diets higher in calories (including fats and simple sugars) and lower in fruits and vegetables are linked with overweight

  - Physical Activity vs. Sedentary Activity - less physical activity and more time spent participating in activities such as watching tv results in less energy expenditure

  - Parental Obesity - children of obese parents are more likely to be overweight themselves. There is an inherited component to childhood overweight that makes it easier for some children to become overweight than others. There are a number of single gene mutations ("genetic alterations") that are capable of causing severe childhood overweight, though these are rare. Even children with genetic risk for overweight will still only become overweight if they consume more calories than they use. Parental obesity may also reflect a family environment that promotes excess eating and insufficient activity.

  - Eating Patterns - skipping meals or failure to maintain a regular eating schedule can result in increased intakes when food is eaten.

  - Parenting Style - some researchers believe that excess parental control over children's eating might lead to poor self regulation of kid's energy intake.

  - Diabetes during pregnancy - overweight and type 2 diabetes occur with greater frequency in the offspring of diabetic mothers (who are also more likely to be obese)

  - Low Birth Weight - Low birth weight (<2500 g) is a risk factor for overweight in several epidemiological studies.

  - Excessive weight gain during pregnancy - Several studies have shown that excessive maternal weight gain during pregnancy is associated with increased birth weight and overweight later in life.

- o Formula Feeding - Breast feeding is generally recommended over formula feeding. Although the exact mechanism in unknown, several long-term studies suggest that breast feeding may prevent excess weight gain as children grow.

- o Parental Eating and Physical Activity Habits - Parents with poor nutritional habits and who lead sedentary lifestyles role model these behaviors for their children, thereby creating an "obesigenic" home environment.

- o Demographic Factors. Certain demographic factors are associated with an increased risk of being overweight in childhood. For example, there is evidence that African-American and Hispanic children 6 to 11 years years old are more likely to be overweight than are non-Hispanic white children of the same age. Asian and Pacific Islander children of the same age were slightly less likely to be overweight.

Measuring Childhood Overweight

Childhood overweight is identified through the measurement of Body Mass Index or BMI. BMI can also be calculated using kilograms (kg) and meters (m), as well as pounds (lbs) and inches (in):

$$BMI = \frac{Weight\ (kg)}{Ht\ (m^2)}$$

$$BMI = \frac{Weight\ (lbs) \times 703}{Ht\ (in^2)}$$

Once BMI is calculated, it can then be used to determine if a child is overweight or not, by comparing the BMI with the CDC growth charts (http://www.cdc.gov/growthcharts/) for children of the same age and sex. Children who have a BMI at or above the 95%, percentile for age and sex are considered overweight. Children with a BMI that falls between the 85%-95% are classified as at risk for overweight.

Parents whose children fall in the "at risk for overweight" category should discuss this with their pediatrician or family physician and should carefully monitor their child's growth. Parents whose children fall in the "overweight" category should make an appointment with their pediatrician or family physician to discuss whether treatment is warranted. Screening for other health risk factors (such as blood pressure or lipid profile) may be recommended by your physician. The BMI is just an initial tool in a series of examinations required to determine if a child is overweight. At no time should a child be diagnosed and labeled overweight by a parent, teacher, or other lay (non-medical) individual. Discussions concerning the child's weight should occur only after reviewing his or her condition with a medical professional.

Pediatricians & Other Health Care Professionals to Facilitate the Prevention of Childhood Overweight (from the American Academy of Pediatrics Policy Statement, August 2003).

Health Supervision Recommendations:

- Identify and track patients at risk by virtue of family history, birth weight, or socioeconomic, ethnic, cultural, or environmental factors.

- Calculate and plot BMI once a year in all children and adolescents.

- Use change in BMI to identify rate of excessive weight gain relative to linear growth.

- Encourage, support, and protect breastfeeding.

- Encourage parents and caregivers to promote healthy eating patterns by offering nutritious snacks, such as vegetables and fruits, low-fat dairy foods, and whole grains; encouraging children's autonomy in self-regulation of food intake and setting appropriate limits on choices; and modeling healthy food choices.

- Routinely promote physical activity, including unstructured play at home, in school, in child care settings, and throughout the community.

- Recommend limitation of television and video time to a maximum of 2 hours per day.

- Recognize and monitor changes in obesity-associated risk factors for adult chronic disease, such as hypertension, dyslipidemia, hyperinsulinemia, impaired glucose tolerance, and symptoms of obstructive sleep apnea syndrome.

- Advocacy Recommendations:

- Help parents, teachers, coaches, and others who influence youth to discuss health habits, not body habitus, as part of their efforts to control overweight.

- Enlist policy makers from local, state, and national organizations and schools to support a healthful lifestyle for all children, including proper diet and adequate opportunity for regular physical activity.

- Encourage organizations that are responsible for health care and health care financing to provide coverage for effective obesity prevention and treatment strategies.

- Encourage public and private sources to direct funding toward research into effective strategies to prevent overweight and to maximize limited family and community resources to achieve healthful outcomes for youth.

- Support and advocate for social marketing intended to promote healthful food choices and increased physical activity.

4.1.4   U.S. Obesity Trends

During the past 20 years there has been a dramatic increase in obesity in the United States. Currently, more than 64% of US adults are either overweight or obese, according to results from the 1999-2000 National Health and Nutrition Examination Survey (NHANES). This figure represents a 14% increase in the prevalence rate from NHANES III (1988-94) and a 36% increase from NHANES II (1976 -80). (Prevalence is the percentage of the population that falls into the designated category.)

The greatest increase took place in the obese group (Body Mass Index > 30), where the prevalence doubled from NHANES II (1976-80).

Roughly 59 million American adults are in this group, which is at the

greatest health risk. (Please note that NHANES data are based on

weights and heights as actually measured by trained health

professionals using standardized measuring equipment.)

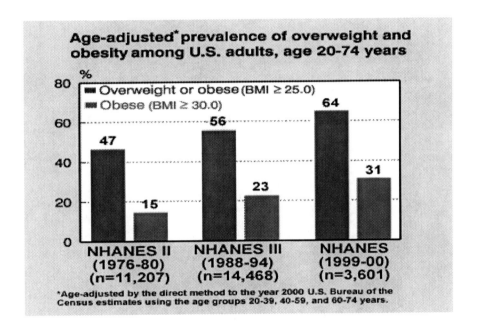

The maps below graphically depict this trend over a 16-year span. It

is important to note that these figures are based on telephone interviews

where weight and height are self-reported. Self reported data tend to

underestimate weight and over-report height. Therefore, the prevalence

rates are actually under-estimates compared to the NHANES data which

originate from actual measurements.

Obesity Trends* Among U.S. Adults
BRFSS, 1985
(*BMI ≥30, or ~ 30 lbs overweight for 5'4" woman)

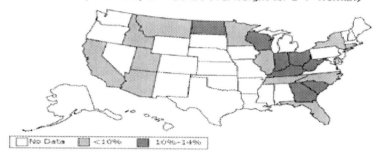

Source: Mokdad A H, et al. *J Am Med Assoc* 1999;282:16, 2001;286:10.

Obesity Trends* Among U.S. Adults
BRFSS, 1993
(*BMI ≥30, or ~ 30 lbs overweight for 5'4" woman)

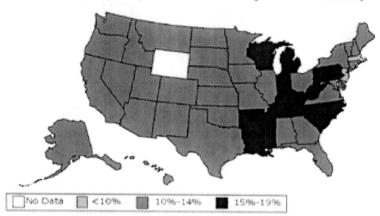

Source: Mokdad A H, et al. *J Am Med Assoc* 1999;282:16, 2001;286:10.

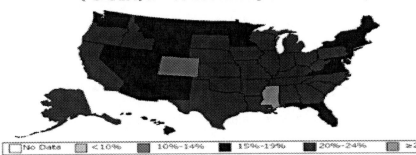

Obesity Trends* Among U.S. Adults
BRFSS, 2001
(*BMI ≥30, or ~ 30 lbs overweight for 5'4" woman)

| No Data | <10% | 10%-14% | 15%-19% | 20%-24% | ≥25% |

Source: Mokdad A H, et al. J Am Med Assoc 1999;282:16, 2001;286:10.

Obesity is associated with significantly increased risk of diabetes mellitus, hypertension, dyslipidemia, certain forms of cancer, sleep apnea, and osteoarthritis. In addition, the increasing prevalence of obesity and its associated complications places a tremendous burden on healthcare utilization and costs. This epidemic of obesity mandates prompt attention from the heath care and preventive health services in order to minimize the rise in the incidence of new case of diabetes, heart disease and other obesity-related complications.

Relationship of BMI to mortality risk

The risks of many medical complications increase with increasing body mass index. These medical complications lead to premature mortality in obese persons. In a prospective study of more than 1 million adults in the United States (457,785 men and 588,369 women), Calle et al studied the relation between body mass index and the risk of death from all causes, cancer, and cardiovascular disease (2). In people who had never smoked, the lowest point of the mortality curve occurred at a body mass index of 23.5 to 24.9 in men and 22.0 to 23.4 in women. Above those points, the relative risk of death increased linearly with increased body mass indices in both men and women. (Appendix C7).

Relationship of overweight and obesity to hypertension

Blood pressure is clearly strongly correlated with BMI. In the INTERSALT study (3), the relationship between body mass index (BMI) and blood pressure was studied in over 10,000 men and women, between 20 and 59 years of age, sampled from 52 centers around the world. BMI was significantly associated with systolic and diastolic blood pressure, independent of age, alcohol intake, smoking habit, and sodium and potassium excretion. The precise prevalence of obesity-related hypertension associated with obesity varies with age, race, and sex of the population studied and with the criteria used for the definition of hypertension and obesity.(4) Roughly 30% of cases of hypertension may be attributable to obesity, and in men under 45 years of age, the figure may be as high as 60%.(5) In the Framingham Offspring Study, 78% of cases of hypertension in men and 64% in women were attributable to obesity.(6)

Prospective studies have shown that obesity increases the risk of developing hypertension.(6)(7) Moreover, weight gain in adulthood is in itself an important risk factor for the development of hypertension.(6)(8) In the long-term Nurses Health Study (8), BMIs at 18 years of age and at midlife were positively associated with the occurrence of hypertension. Weight gain after 18 years of age significantly increased the risk for hypertension. Compared with women who gained less than 2 kg (4.4 pounds), women who gained 5.0 to 9.9 kg (11-22 pounds) were 74% more likely to have hypertension, and those who gained more than 25 kg (55 pounds) were more than 5 times more likely to have hypertension. (7) Excess weight and even modest adult weight gain substantially increase risk for hypertension: each 1-kg increase in weight after age 18 was associated with a 5% increase in risk for hypertension.

Relationship of overweight and obesity to type 2 diabetes

It is likely that the 25% increase in the prevalence of diabetes in the last 20 years in the United States (9) is due to the marked increase in the prevalence of obesity. Body mass index, abdominal fat distribution, and weight gain are important risk factors for type 2 diabetes mellitus. Data from NHANES III indicated that two-thirds of adult men and women in the United States diagnosed with type 2 diabetes have a BMI of 27 kg/m² or greater.(10) Moreover, the risk of diabetes increased with BMI;

diabetes prevalence was 2%, 8% and 13% in those with BMI 25-

29.9kg/m² (overweight), 30-34.9 kg/m² (class 1 obesity), and >35 kg/m²

(class 2 and 3 obesity), respectively.(9) Data from the Nurses Health

Study demonstrated that the risk of diabetes begins to increase in

"normal" weight women when BMI exceeds 22 kg/m².(11)(12) Weight

gain during adulthood also increases the risk of diabetes, even at

relatively low levels of BMI in initially normal weight individuals.(12)(13)

Compared with women who kept their weight within 5 kg (11 pounds) of

their initial weight over a 14-year period, women who gained only 5 to 8

kg (11-17.6 pounds) were nearly twice as likely to develop diabetes over

that period, even after adjusting for initial BMI. Those who gained 11 to

20 kg (about 24 to 44 pounds) were more than 5 times as likely to

develop diabetes. (N.A.S.O. 2003). Adapted with permission from

Children's Eating, Laboratory, Copyright 2001; The Pennsylvania State

University. (Appendix C8).

4.2 Federal Trade Commission Targets Media

Federal Trade Commission, "Consumer Report", November 9, 2004,

the FTC launched "Operation Big Fat Lie," a nation-wide law enforcement

sweep against six companies making false weight-loss claims in national

advertisements. Operation Big Fat Lie is the latest in the Commission's efforts to: stop deceptive advertising and provide refunds to consumers harmed by unscrupulous weight-loss advertisers; encourage media outlets not to carry advertisements containing bogus weight-loss claims; and educate consumers to be on their guard against companies promising miraculous weight loss without diet or exercise.

Complaints in each of the six cases announced today allege that defendants used at least one of the seven bogus weight-loss claims that are part of the FTC's "Red Flag" education campaign announced in December 2003. That ongoing Red Flag campaign provides guidance to assist media outlets in voluntarily screening out weight-loss ads that contain claims that are too good to be true.

"False and misleading advertisements are about as credible as a note from the Tooth Fairy," said Federal Trade Commission Chairman Deborah Platt Majoras. "As part of our 'no tolerance' policy, we are announcing six new cases against advertisers using bogus weight loss claims. By also working with media outlets to reject false ads and educating consumers to make informed choices, the FTC hopes to keep this national obesity epidemic from getting worse."

The cases challenge ads containing false Red Flag claims for a variety of products, including pills, powders, green tea, topical gels, and diet patches. The FTC alleges in each case that the weight-loss claims are false and that the defendants did not have adequate substantiation for the claims they made. The challenged ads ran in nationally-known publications such as: Cosmopolitan; Woman's Own; Complete Woman; USA Weekend; Dallas Morning News; San Francisco Chronicle; Cleveland Plain Dealer; Albuquerque Journal; and in Spanish-language publications, such as TeleRevista Magazine. In each of these cases, the Commission is seeking to stop the bogus ads and to secure redress for consumers. In addition to these cases, the Commission has filed lawsuits against seven other companies since April 2004 for making similarly false Red Flag weight-loss claims.

1. FTC's "Red Flag" Media Education Campaign

These cases follow up on the FTC's December 2003 announcement of its Red Flag initiative to encourage the media to adopt standards that would screen out weight-loss advertisements that contain false claims. Preliminary results of this effort are promising. "Through monitoring, we have seen a decrease in the frequency of false weight loss claims in the media," said Chairman Majoras. "This tells us that many in the publishing and broadcasting industries are doing the right thing and stepping up their efforts to reject ads targeting the insecurity and weakness of unsuspecting buyers. That is good for consumers, good for the media, and good for honest advertisers."

As part of the Red Flag initiative, the FTC staff has sent reminder letters to media outlets that ran advertisements challenged in the six law enforcement actions. The purpose of these letters are to assist media in identifying and rejecting weight-loss ads that contain facially false claims. The media letters include: (1) a copy of the problem advertisement; (2) a copy of the Commission's Reference Guide for Media on Bogus Weight Loss Claim Detection; and (3) a description of each Red Flag Claim contained in the problem advertisement.

2. Consumer Education

The FTC launched a campaign to help consumers spot claims that almost always signal a diet rip-off. Weighing the Evidence in Diet Ads warns consumers to steer clear of diet pills, patches, creams, or other products that offer quick weight loss without diet or exercise; that claim to block the absorption of fat, calories, or carbohydrates; or that promise that consumers can eat all they want of high-calorie foods and still lose weight. Consumers can find more tips on protecting themselves from questionable diet products at http://www.ftc.gov/dietfit.

The FTC has also launched a new "teaser" web site to reach consumers surfing online for weight-loss products. Teaser sites mimic real Web pages, using common buzz words and making the kind of exaggerated diet claims found on many web sites. At first glance, the teaser site appears to advertise a new pill promising to help consumers "Lose up to 10 pounds per week – with no sweat, no starvation!" Once the consumers try to order the product, they learn the ad is actually a consumer education piece posted by the FTC to warn consumers about diet rip-offs. The FTC's new teaser site can be found at: http://www.wemarket4u.net/fatfoe.

3. Law Enforcement Actions

Selfworx.com LLC

On November 4, 2004, the Commission filed a complaint in the U.S. District Court, District of Maine, against Selfworx.com LLC, Iworx LLC, and Jeffrey V. Kral. The Scarborough, Maine-based defendants advertised two weight-loss products: gel•ä•thin – a topical gel, and Ultra LipoLean – a dietary supplement tablet described as a "fat blocker."

The complaint alleges that the defendants make false and unsubstantiated claims that gel•ä•thin, when rubbed into the skin: (1)

causes substantial weight loss, including as much as 21 pounds in six weeks; (2) dissolves fat deposits in days; and (3) dissolves and removes cellulite from the body. The complaint further alleges that defendants falsely claim that clinical studies demonstrate that gel•ä•thin will reduce fat and cellulite deposits on contact.

The complaint further alleges that the defendants make false and unsubstantiated claims that LipoLean causes rapid and substantial weight loss, including as much as four pounds per week, without the need to diet; and that only two tablets of LipoLean absorb 20 to 30 grams of fat from a meal.

4. Femina, Inc.

On November 8, 2004, the FTC filed a complaint in the U.S. District Court, Southern District of Florida, against Femina, Inc., based in Pembroke Pines, Florida, and its owner, Husnain Mirza, challenging ads for three products – "1-2-3 Reduce Fat" (a three-part kit), "Siluette Patch" (a transdermal patch made from pure seaweed), and "Fat Seltzer Reduce" (a dietary supplement). The 1-2-3 Reduce Fat kit includes Xena RX, a diet pill; Reduce Gel Magic, a gel to put on the body; and a plaster corset to wrap around the body. The Xena RX pill purportedly contains green tea extract, and the Magic gel purportedly contains aloe vera and sea algae. The defendants primarily use Spanish-language ads.

The complaint alleges that the defendants make false and unsubstantiated claims: (1) that 1-2-3 Reduce Fat causes weight loss by blocking and eliminating fat; (2) that the green tea extract blocks up to 40 percent of the absorption of fat; and (3) that the aloe vera and seaweed gel eliminates inches of fat.

The complaint also alleges that the defendants make false and unsubstantiated claims that the Siluette Patch: (1) causes substantial weight loss when worn on the body; (2) causes rapid weight loss with no dietary changes; (3) eliminates cellulite and controls metabolism; and (4) eliminates accumulated fat.

The complaint also alleges that the defendants make false and unsubstantiated claims that Fat Seltzer Reduce: (1) causes rapid and permanent weight loss; (2) causes fat to be absorbed and eliminated fast and easily through the urine; and (3) causes weight loss without the need to diet or exercise.

On November 8, 2004, the court entered a temporary restraining order that prohibits the defendants from making false or misleading claims for any weight loss product. The TRO also includes provisions requiring the defendants to maintain records and other evidence, and requiring them to provide an accounting of their sales and other financial information.

5. CHK Trading Co., Inc.

On November 4, 2004, the FTC filed a complaint in the U.S. District Court, Southern District of New York, against two companies – CHK Trading Co., Inc., based in New Jersey, and CHK Trading Corp., based in New York City. The Commission alleged that the corporate defendants and their principal, Chong Kim, market and sell "Hanmeilin Cellulite Cream," a topical cream which contains Chinese herbs and other all-natural ingredients. Users are told to apply the cream on the buttocks, stomach, and thighs and massage until the cream is completely absorbed. The defendants advertise their product to Spanish-speaking consumers via national advertisements in TeleRevista magazine, as well as to English-speaking and Korean-speaking consumers via their Web sites.

The complaint alleges that the defendants make false and unsubstantiated claims that rubbing Hanmeilin Cellulite Cream into the body: (1) causes permanent weight loss; (2) causes substantial weight loss, including as much as 10 to 95 pounds; and (3) eliminates fat and cellulite.

6. Natural Products

On November 3, 2004, the FTC filed a complaint in the U.S. District
Court, Central District of California, against Natural Products, LLC; All
Natural 4 U, LLC; and Ana M. Solkamans. The Tustin, California-based
defendants sell a dietary supplement called "Bio Trim," "Body-Trim/Bio-
Trim" or "Body-Trim" in capsule and powder form. Users are told to take
two capsules with eight ounces of water one half-hour before their two
biggest meals, or, if using the powder, users are told to take one half-
teaspoon of the powder mix in eight ounces of cold juice 15 minutes
before two meals.

The complaint alleges that the defendants make false and
unsubstantiated claims that Bio Trim: (1) causes users to lose substantial
weight, while eating unlimited amounts of food; (2) causes substantial
weight loss by blocking the absorption of fat or calories; (3) works for all
overweight users; and (4) is clinically proven to cause rapid and
substantial weight loss without reducing calories.

7. New England Diet Center

On November 4, 2004, the Commission filed a complaint in the U.S.
District Court, District of Connecticut, against Bronson Partners, LLC,

(doing business as New England Diet Center and Bronson Day Spa), and Martin Howard. The defendants, based in Westport, Connecticut, sold Chinese Diet Tea and the Bio-Slim Patch – purported weight loss products. Users of the Chinese Diet Tea are told to drink one cup of tea after each meal to neutralize the absorption of fattening foods.

The complaint alleges that the defendants make false and unsubstantiated claims that Chinese Diet Tea: (1) causes rapid and substantial weight loss without the need to diet or exercise; (2) enables users to lose as much as six pounds per week over multiple weeks and months without the need to diet or exercise; (3) enables users to lose substantial weight while enjoying their favorite foods; (4) blocks the absorption of fat and calories; and (5) causes substantial weight loss for all users. The complaint further alleges that defendants falsely claim that Chinese Diet Tea is clinically proven to cause rapid and substantial weight loss without exercising or dieting.

The complaint further alleges that the defendants make false and unsubstantiated claims that the Bio-Slim Patch: (1) causes rapid and substantial weight loss without the need to exercise or diet; and (2) causes substantial weight loss when worn on the body.

8. AVS Marketing, Inc.

On October 27, 2004, the FTC filed a complaint in U.S. District Court for the Northern District of Illinois, Eastern Division, against AVS Marketing, Inc., and William R. Heid. The defendants, based in Thomson, Illinois, sell "Himalayan Diet Breakthrough," a dietary supplement containing Nepalese Mineral Pitch – "a paste-like material" that "oozes out of the cliff face cracks in the summer season" in the Himalayas. Users are directed to take one tablet with water before lunch, dinner and bedtime.

The complaint alleges that the defendants make false and unsubstantiated claims that Himalayan Diet Breakthrough: (1) causes rapid and substantial weight loss, including as much as 37 pounds in 8 weeks, without the need to reduce caloric intake or increase exercise; (2) causes users to lose substantial weight, including as much as 37 pounds in 8 weeks, while still consuming unlimited amounts of food; (3) causes substantial weight loss, including as much as 37 pounds in 8 weeks, by preventing the formation of body fat; (4) causes substantial weight loss for all users; and (5) enables users to lose safely as much as 37 pounds in 8 weeks.

On October 28, 2004, the court entered a temporary restraining order that prohibits the defendants from making the above claims or any other false or unsubstantiated product claims, and prohibits further sales of Himalayan Diet Breakthrough pending determination of the FTC's motion for a preliminary injunction. The TRO also includes provisions freezing the defendants' assets, requiring the defendants to maintain records and other evidence, and requiring the defendants to provide an accounting of their sales and other financial information.

4.2.1 State Enforcement Action

The Commission was joined today by the Maine Attorney General's Office, which is filing an additional weight loss enforcement action in Maine state court against a diet patch seller from that state. The defendant in that case made false claims for two weight-loss products – Slim Patch and Bodylite Gel Patch. The ads appeared in advertising carried in newspapers across the United States.

The Commission vote authorizing staff to file the six complaints in the appropriate federal district court was 5-0.

NOTE: The Commission files a complaint when it has "reason to believe" that the law has been or is being violated, and it appears to the Commission that a proceeding is in the public interest. A complaint is not a finding or ruling that the defendant has actually violated the law. Each case will be decided by the court.

The FTC's Consumer Response Center, Room 130, 600 Pennsylvania Avenue, N.W., Washington, D.C. 20580. The FTC works for the consumer to prevent fraudulent, deceptive, and unfair business practices in the marketplace and to provide information to help consumers spot, stop, and avoid them.

4.3 Youth Industry Analysis

Thanks to teens' enormous and growing consumer power - they spent $175 billion in 2003 - the age group is more than enticing. And teens are trend-obsessed. Yet their preoccupation with the "next big thing" can be a double-edged sword.

Young people are particularly receptive to messages that promise either a new experience or one that satisfies a need-state that's unique to this age group. But they're also adept at blocking out messages they deem false or misdirected. Brands that over promise, under deliver or falter even slightly in an ad's tone or execution are often shocked to learn just how unforgiving teens can be.

For example, a couple of years ago it was nearly impossible to escape the word "extreme." The term gained popularity as a way to describe action sports that favored adrenaline and independence over teamwork and tradition. Before long, marketers seized on the "extreme" lifestyle as a way to convey their brands as youthful, daring and rebellious.

Although such imagery was a natural fit for athletic-related brands, the lifestyle's focus on fitness and activity made high-calorie snack foods and soft drinks somewhat less appropriate candidates. Still, such products frequently promised increased energy or a "flavor rush" that teens accepted as sufficiently powerful to justify the "extreme" descriptor.

By the time shampoo and toothpaste hopped on the extreme bandwagon, teens concluded that these products had not only showed up late to the party, they'd barged into the wrong place entirely. Such marketing gaffes damage "brand cred." And the damage isn't always limited to those guilty of misdirected marketing. Once teens deemed that the corporate world had co-opted the fiercely independent "extreme" spirit, nearly all attempts to market under that banner became suspect.

As marketers become more youth-savvy, they logically keep an ever-keener eye trained on emerging trends. This attention often results in an abbreviated life cycle for many trends. Typically, the teens responsible for establishing and broadcasting trends don't want to be part of the mainstream; they value their position either at the top of the trend-adoption hierarchy or outside of it entirely. As marketers aggressively mine youth culture, trends move more quickly into the mainstream. In turn, those teens who first established the trend abandon it and move on to something else. It's a catch-22: As "cool" becomes more sought-after, it also becomes more fleeting.

Rather than simply chasing after the latest and greatest, marketers advocate a more holistic approach. They prefer to help clients discover the nuances of how teens regard their brand: what young consumers expect of it and where else the brand can take them, including how to leverage trends that fit with and appropriately add to their brands.

The key is to turn the pursuit of trends into a powerful, brand-fortifying strategy, rather than a costly red herring.

4.3.1 <u>Youth Industry Home Décor</u>

In surveys done by Teen Vogue and by Teenage Research Unlimited, young people say they get their spending money from chores, baby-sitting, weekly allowances, presents from relatives and from time-to-time, parents willing to help out on big expenditures. More retailers are rushing to take advantage of what has become a $17 billion market for room furnishings meant to appeal directly to young people from third grade through high school. It is a market, said Michael Wood, a vice president at Teenage Research Unlimited, that has "really exploded in the last two years."

Instead of leaving furnishing decisions to their parents, older teenagers and their 8- to 14-year-old sisters and brothers -- called tweens by retailers -- are proud, insistent even, about making those decisions themselves.

Last year, teenagers and tweens spent an average of $386 to decorate their rooms -- more than double the figure of a decade ago, according to the Wonder Group, a youth-marketing company in Cincinnati.

Merchants are responding. Besides Dry Ice, a $30 million private company that started on a mall cart and has grown to 40 stores from 7 in the last three years, this market is full of start-ups, some more successful than others.

Paul Frank began five years ago by making wallets in a garage. He now sells sheets and pillowcases emblazoned with primitive monkey heads. As Paul Frank Industries, he puts out a brochure of home bedding for tweens, featuring the monkey heads and skeleton heads. The company has 13 stores, as well as a fast-growing wholesale business supplying department stores and specialty shops.

A year ago, Pottery Barn opened PBTeen's Web site, full of flokati rugs and hanging shelves. Last week, the PB Teen site recorded 117,000 visitors; a spokeswoman said retail stores were coming next. Two years ago, this consumer was not addressed at all," said Patrick Wynhoff, the senior vice president at PBTeen. "Teens had to find stuff for their rooms in Ikea or Target or adult furniture shops or do their own makeshift improvisations. Now everybody's hopping on the wagon."

Limited Too, after a debacle with its stand-alone Mishmash furnishings and accessories stores for teenagers, is at it again with a new chain called Justice, for a younger clientele: ages 7 to 14. The company has already opened 33 stores, with dozens more planned for next year.

The best-selling item? A $7 privacy door bell, which parents, older siblings and other would-be visitors must ring before entering.

In the last year, "Trading Spaces" the popular television reality show, has spun off "Trading Spaces: Boys vs. Girls." In one episode, a 12-year-old boy pronounced a pink room disgusting and vowed to do better; a recent show pitted Andrew vs. Caitlin, in a battle over playrooms.

Tweens and teenagers are not easy to figure out, as retailers unabashedly admit. But one thing is clear, those who survey them say: parents have a lot less influence over what they buy and how they furnish their rooms than they once did.

Eileen Joyce, the vice president for interior design at Bloomingdale's, who has been in this line of work for 25 years, says children are more involved in their rooms than ever before. "The parents used to figure it out and tell the kids," she said. "Now they ask the children, What would you like?"

Ms. Joyce said that teenagers and their tween siblings often have starkly differing tastes. "A 17-year-old girl might want ruffles and canopies," she said, while "the 13- and 14-year-olds tend to want platform beds, very modern, very sleek."

"There's a definite switch from Pottery Barn Kids, where Mom makes the choices, with maybe a little input," Mr. Wynhoff of PBTeen said. Next year, he said, PBTeen plans to introduce an "item of their dreams" feature, which will allow kids to lobby for their deepest desires by making a list of chores they will do to earn money to pay for what they want -- or the movies and candy they will forgo.

Mr. Wynhoff, while refusing to break out sales separately for PBTeen, said the unit, which is part of the $3 billion Williams-Sonoma Company, had "exceeded all of our expectations consistently."

Pollsters and retailers say this age group is continually gaining sophistication. Not only are many girls mini-fashionist, but both boys and girls say they watch adult-oriented shows about houses and interior design.

In a survey done by Lowe's, the home-improvement chain, 65 percent of teenagers said they had watched home makeover television shows like "Trading Spaces," "This Old House" and "Cribs."

According to MarketResearch.com, these young sophisticates represent a potentially vast audience with considerable buying power. There are 23 million Americans ages 6 to 14, and 32 million from ages 12 to 19. The number of teenagers alone has risen 16.6 percent since 1990. They have more to say about how the entire house is furnished. They have begun to exert influence on the rest of the family.

The winner is a monthly article where a teenage reader describes how she decorated - and, usually, says she is constantly redecorating -- her own living quarters in the family's house.

4.3.2 <u>Teen Style Change</u>

Just a year ago the average college sophomore was just another grungy teenager, with his long hair, dirty jeans and favorite black T-shirt with a gory red bird on the front. Now he is transformed. He has cut his hair, and in a couple of weeks, he plans to go shopping for some blue button-down shirts.   He threw away the 4-letter word t-shirts and is now going for the Gap and Landsend look. "The Grunge" is fading.

Young people are getting more sophisticated, or maybe they are just getting bored. But from kindergarten to college, America's students are cleaning up their acts. And while they do not generally want their fall fashions to be labeled "preppy" - they insist they are putting their own twist on the look - they say styles are definitely getting simpler.

Goth is also out. The numbers have plummeted at Hot Topic, a clothing chain that was the darling of the spooky, blood-and-darkness Goth crowd. American Eagle Outfitters, meanwhile, whose figures fell as Hot Topic's rose, is suddenly soaring, with its stripped-down, cleaned-up khakis flying out the door; July sales were 22 percent higher than they were last year. And Polo Ralph Lauren, whose expensive children's clothes are the epitome of prep, just reported that profits more than doubled from a year ago.

Students polled have reported that they have kissed grunge goodbye. "That punk look is going away, all those bracelets up the arm. Black and pink is out, and those shirts that say, 'Funky Monkey.' " Chic geek is the latest transition.

Merchants call the new style "classic" or "retro" - just not "contemporary," which now translates as too baggy or too tight, too low-slung and too low-cut. Students are "taking themselves a little more seriously; they're thinking a little more of the image they're projecting," said John D. Morris, a retail analyst who holds focus groups with teenagers in malls around the country. "It's a backlash to what was sexy, what was distressed or dirty or grungy. Now they say that look is too affected."

In case that sounds too Pollyanna-ish to believe, another analyst is hearing the same thing from students, but with a subtext that suggests their motives are more refined - and more manipulative.

"This year's kids seem much more sophisticated, savvy," said Marshal Cohen, chief researcher with the NPD Group in Port Washington, N.Y., "and they are telling their parents they'll buy this preppy stuff because it will last three or four years - and then arguing that with the extra money the parents will save, they can buy them high-speed Internet for $40 a month. Or maybe a digital camera."

Mr. Morris agrees that there is more wheeling and dealing going on. "It's all about responsibility this season," he said. "They'll argue that a cell phone is justified for security reasons. And they will say they need to have access to the Internet; that it is required for schoolwork."

With that kind of maturity, who wants cleavage?

Michael Wood, the vice president of Teenage Research Unlimited in Northbrook, Ill., said the young people he surveys say they are simply sick of what is in their closets. "They're notoriously fickle," Mr. Wood said, "and they've moved on to something new. The last several years, necklines and waists were going lower and lower and showing more and more skin, and they realized you can't go any lower or show any more. The pendulum swung."

Although the preppy look may seem old hat to many parents, Mr. Wood, who said he surveyed teenagers daily, said that it is fresh to young people, who may think they "discovered" the style in thrift shops. Like other pollsters and merchants, Mr. Wood said that few teenagers would do preppy head-to-toe. "They'll wear the polo shirts with the collars turned up, with the surf or skate, or both, in a smorgasbord of styles."

Indeed, turned-up collars seem to be in vogue again - even turned-up jacket collars. On Thursday, Nathan Watters, 19, from St. Louis, stood on a SoHo street corner and modeled his latest purchase: a charcoal gray corduroy blazer he had just bought at French Connection for $168. "I just pop the collar - like this," he said, posing for a photographer. Jeans are still big, he added, as his three friends nodded. "Cut is still O.K., but neat," he said. (Rozhorn, 2004)

4.3.3 The Shopping Mall Industry Takes Responsibility

It's 10 o'clock "Do you know where your teen is?"   Many shopping centers across the country, has a curfew for unchaperoned teens. The witching hour is 9:30 p.m. At other malls, the curfew is as early as 6 p.m.

Teens hate it but, parents support it. These establishments must suppress their level of greed and balance it with responsibility for their young consumer's safety.

The mall, for many teens, is more than a place to spend money — it's a place to see and be seen, a place to entertain themselves, sometimes just a place to escape Mom's nagging.

"Teens don't really feel like there's a lot of places for them. They don't want to hang out at home. They can't go to a bar or nightclub, obviously," said Rob Callender, senior trends manager for Teen Research Unlimited, a marketing research firm.

Some malls set curfews after fights broke out among unruly teens; at other centers, it was a way to unclog the hallways for paying customers.

"Hanging out in large groups, that is what we're not looking for," said Jim Craycroft, the facilities manager at Newport on the Levee in Newport, Ky., across the Ohio River from Cincinnati. The mall requires escorts after 8 p.m. except for teens going directly to a movie theater. The International Council of Shopping Centers does not keep track of how many of the country's 46,990 malls and shopping centers have curfews, but they are enforced at malls in not only Kentucky and Ohio, but also Minnesota, New

York, Pennsylvania, Missouri, Georgia, Tennessee, North Carolina and the number is increasing every day.

According to Teenage Research Unlimited, 68 percent of 12- to 19-year-olds spend time at the mall in any given week. On average, teens spend 3 1/2 hours at the mall each week.

The Mall of America in suburban Minneapolis, the country's largest retail and entertainment center, began its "parental escort policy" in 1996.

"They like to hang out in big groups, they like to see their friends, but then customers couldn't walk through the hallways," said Maureen Bausch, the mall's vice president of business development.

Teens 15 and younger must be accompanied by a parent or guardian 21 or older after 6 p.m. Fridays and Saturdays. One adult can escort up to 10 children. In the year before the curfew went into effect, Mall of America had about 300 incidents involving youths under 16 that required mall officials to either issue trespassing citations or call police. The year after the policy was put into place, there were two incidents, Bausch said.

"You don't just say you're not welcome because they are welcome," she said. "We just welcome them with a parent," she said.

Mall of America had about 10,000 youths under 16 on any Friday or Saturday night before the policy, Bausch said. Now, there are even more shoppers on those nights.

Some retailers at Easton said the rule helps them maintain a more professional atmosphere. "A curfew benefits retailers mainly because we don't have a bunch of kids running around," said Matt Radici, 23, who works at the mall's T-Mobile cell phone store. "There's a lot of loitering, and cell phones are such a fashion item that they'll take the model phones, the plastic ones that don't work, because they think they're cool," he said.

Some teens welcome curfews. Because of safety. They prefer the atmosphere of the mall because it has everything they need since the under 16 year olds normally don't have cars. They can shop, eat, go to the movies and engage in all the cool happenings. (Chang, 2004)

4.3.4 Valuable, but painful lessons

Millions of dollars are spent annually by manufacturers of everything from breakfast cereal to hot rods. All trying to out think the next move of today's youth. Experts are of the mind that youths today have but, one think on their mind – "Consumption". To put it in real time perspective Teenagers fear they could be drafted for service in a war and worry that another terrorist attack is likely They give the president--and their parents--high marks for their responses to the events of 911 in 2001 on the United States.

Teenagers are closely following the news and learning real-life lessons about conflicts in the Middle East, whose countries have suddenly burst alive from dry textbooks, according to interviews and a national survey recently released. They wonder how could we be so cocky and arrogant to think this could never happen to us again. Eighty-five percent of 190 teenagers surveyed said they believe their lives will be different because of the Sept. 11 attacks on the World Trade Center and the Pentagon, according to Teenage Research Unlimited, a Northbrook-based market research firm.

Mostly, the teens' thoughts mirrored those of their parents and other adults. The initial shock and disbelief has transformed into a sort of numbness and has stirred feelings of patriotism. "It kind of shook my faith in how you just walk around and never feel like anything will happen in America," said Sara Semelka, 17, a senior at Lyons Township High School in La Grange, who added, though, that she feels safe at school. As editor of her school's newspaper, The Lion, she has been juggling her own feelings while scrambling to assign stories that will be relevant to classmates who will be making life changing decisions by the end of the school year.

"Whenever I've seen on the news bombing and rubble, it seemed disconnected from me and my life, and I thought I'd never have to face that all," Semelka said. "I'm feeling now like no one is really immune to that. It will always be a little bit in the back of my mind."

"Reality set in," he said. "I still have the SATs, the ACTs and grades to worry about, but something is different. There is so much more to life right now than what the cool kids are wearing at the mall".

The teenagers also sensed some hypocrisy in the widespread displays of patriotism and people capitalizing on it to force yet another purchase. "If you didn't have a flag in your window before, you shouldn't have one up now," said Terrance Spencer, 17, of Evanston.

According to the survey, 75 percent of teens polled believe another terrorist attack is somewhat or very likely to occur and sixty-eight percent believe President Bush is doing a good or excellent job in responding. Amid their normal routines of classes, homework and planning homecoming dances, the teenagers are hashing over U.S. military policy and raising money to help victims.

Some teens acknowledged that they are of a largely materialistic generation enriched by sophisticated technology but unfamiliar with war and would like to see more dollars spent on their safety and understanding of the future of their safety as opposed to if they'll be wearing their pants on their waist or hips this season.

Topics regarding the draft are creeping into this teen generation's forethoughts. Hopes that the draft will remain voluntary. When asked for a show of hands from students who would enlist if asked to do so - Less than a third raised their hands. New Trier sees 95 percent of its graduating seniors go on to college.   One 17 year old male student, of Edgewater, a Loyola Academy senior, said that if his country called for it, he'd go to war. Reluctantly. But he said he has found one good thing out of the horror, and other teens echoed his sentiment. They are surprised, and impressed, with the way their peers have reacted. And they want it known that most young people are not acting apathetic or spoiled as the stereotypes suggest. The teens are learning and conversing about world developments in a big way.

"Before this, the Middle East was one big region to me. I didn't know everything that was going on, or who was who," Smith said. "This is something that's really struck home with people. I guess it shows as we get older, we do start to care more and do know more about what's going on." (Black and Vogt, 2003).

CHAPTER 5

SUMMARY, CONCLUSIONS & RECOMMENDATIONS

"The survival of democracy depends on the ability of large numbers of people to make realistic choices in the light of adequate information. A dictatorship, on the other hand, maintains itself by censoring or distorting the facts, and by appealing, not to reason, not to enlightened self-interest, but, to passion and prejudice... after all, it may be argued capitalism is dead, **consumerism** is king, and **consumerism** requires the services of expert salesmen versed in all the arts, including the more insidious arts of persuasion." (Aldous Huxley, 1998)

Government Interventions

Advertising is indeed protected by the First Amendment of the U.S. Constitution. Advertising or "Commercial speech" enjoys somewhat less

First Amendment protection from governmental encroachment than other types of speech. The Federal Trade Commission, for example, may regulate speech that is found to be "deceptive."

Under the landmark U.S. Supreme Court decision, Central Hudson Gas & Electric Corp. v. Public Service Commission Of New York, No. 79-565, Supreme Court Of The United States, 447 U.S. 557; 100 S. Ct. 2343; 1980 U.S. LEXIS 48; 65 L. Ed. 2d 341; 6 Media L. Rep. 1497; 34 P.U.R.4th 178, June 20, 1980, a state must justify restrictions on truthful, non-misleading commercial speech by demonstrating that its actions "directly advance" a substantial state interest and are no more extensive than necessary to serve that interest. This is the so-called **Central Hudson Test.**

Commercial speech now clearly has prominent place in the rights protected by the First Amendment. A 1993 Supreme Court opinion summarized the general principles underlying the protection of commercial speech:

The commercial market place, like other spheres of our social and cultural life, provides a forum where ideas and information flourish. Some of the ideas and information are vital, some of slight worth. But the general rule is that the speaker and the audience, not the government, assess the value of the information presented. Thus, even a communication that does no more than propose a commercial transaction is entitled to the coverage of the First Amendment." (Edenfield v. Fane, 123 L. Ed. 2d 543, 113 S. Ct. 1792, 1798 (1993).)

At one time, purely commercial advertisements were considered to be outside the First Amendment's protection. The Constitution imposes no restraint on the government as to the regulation of "purely commercial advertising".

While the U.S. Supreme Court has often acknowledged this constitutional protection, the Supreme Court's decisions have recognized the "'common sense' distinction between speech proposing a commercial transaction, which occurs in an area traditionally subject to government regulation, and other varieties of speech."

These distinctions have led the Court to conclude that "the Constitution . . . affords a lesser protection to commercial speech than to other constitutionally guaranteed expression." U.S. v. Edge Broadcasting Co.

Trustees v. Fox, 1989; Central Hudson Gas & Electric Corp. v. Public Service Com. 1980. In Central Hudson, the Supreme Court set out the important four-part test for assessing government restrictions on commercial speech:

First, the commercial speech] at least must concern lawful activity and not be misleading. Next, we ask whether the asserted governmental interest is substantial. If both inquiries yield positive answers, we must determine whether the regulation directly advances the governmental interest asserted, and whether it is not more extensive than is necessary to serve that interest."

This four-part analysis endured to this day as the constitutional benchmark in commercial speech cases.

Congress enacted the Lanham Act "to protect persons engaged in such commerce against unfair competition." 15 U.S.C. Section 1127. Section 43(a) of the Lanham Act provides in relevant part that:

"Any person who . . . uses in commerce any . . . false or misleading description of fact, or false or misleading representation of fact, which in commercial advertising or promotion, misrepresents the nature, characteristics, qualities, or geographic origin of his or her or another person's goods, services, or commercial activities, shall be liable in a civil action by any person who believes that he or she is likely to be damaged by such act." 15 U.S.C. Section 1125(a)(1)(B).

This section provides protection against a 'myriad of deceptive commercial practices,' including false advertising or promotion." (Resource Developers v. Statue of Liberty-Ellis Island Found., 926 F.2d

134, 139 (2d Cir.1991).) Section 43(a) of the Lanham Act has been characterized as a remedial statute that should be broadly construed.

To sustain an action under Section 43(a) a plaintiff must allege:

(1) that the defendant has or that there is likelihood of injury to the plaintiff. The Lanham Act does not define either "advertising" or "promotion." Nor is the Act's legislative history addresses only the requirement that the advertising or promotion be "commercial" in nature. The Court pointed out that the "`commercial'" requirement was inserted to ensure that Section 43(a) does not infringe on free speech protected by the First Amendment." The Court concluded that the advertisement in this case is clearly commercial in nature.

In order for representations to constitute "commercial advertising or promotion" under Section 43(a)(1)(B), they must be:

- commercial speech

- must be disseminated sufficiently to the relevant purchasing public

  to constitute " advertising" or "promotion" within that industry.

Industry Interventions

The Marketing Association's Guidelines for Ethical Business
Practice are intended to provide individuals and organizations involved in
marketing in all media with generally accepted principles of conduct.
These guidelines reflect The DMA's long-standing policy of high levels of
ethics and the responsibility of the Association, its members, and all
marketers to maintain consumer and community relationships that are
based on fair and ethical principles. In addition to providing general
guidance to the industry, the Guidelines for Ethical Business Practice are
used by The DMA's Committee on Ethical Business Practice and the
Teleservices Ethics Committee, industry peer review committees, as the
standard to which direct marketing promotions that are the subject of
complaint to The DMA are compared.

These self-regulatory guidelines are intended to be honored in light
of their aims and principles. All marketers should support the guidelines in
spirit and not treat their provisions as obstacles to be circumvented by
legal ingenuity.

These guidelines also represent The DMA's general philosophy that
self-regulatory measures are preferable to governmental mandates. Self-
regulatory actions are more readily adaptable to changing techniques and

economic and social conditions. They encourage widespread use of sound business practices.

Because dishonest, misleading or offensive communications discredit all means of advertising and marketing, including direct marketing, observance of these guidelines by all concerned is expected. All persons involved in marketing and advertising should take reasonable steps to encourage other industry members to follow these guidelines as well. (DMA, 2004)

Marketing to Children and Teens

Article #13

Offers and the manner in which they are presented that are suitable for adults only should not be made to children. In determining the suitability of a communication with children online or in any other medium, marketers should address the age range, knowledge, sophistication and maturity of their intended audience.

PARENTAL RESPONSIBILITY AND CHOICE

Article #14

Marketers should provide notice and an opportunity to opt out of the marketing process so that parents have the ability to limit the collection, use and disclosure of their children's names, addresses or other personally identifiable information.

INFORMATION FROM OR ABOUT CHILDREN

Article #15

Marketers should take into account the age range, knowledge, sophistication and maturity of children when collecting information from them. Marketers should limit the collection, use and dissemination of information collected from or about children to information required for the promotion, sale and delivery of goods and services, provision of customer services. Any information collected from a child should be available for parents review upon request. , Marketers should effectively explain that the information is being requested for marketing purposes. Information not appropriate for marketing purposes should not be collected.

Marketers should implement strict security measures to ensure against unauthorized access, alteration or dissemination of the data collected from or about children.

MARKETING ONLINE TO

CHILDREN UNDER 13 YEARS OF AGE

Article #16

Marketers should not collect personally identifiable information online from a child under 13 without prior parental consent or direct parental notification of the nature and intended use of such information online and an opportunity for the parent to prevent such use and participation in the activity. Online contact information should only be used to directly respond to an activity initiated by a child and not to re-contact a child for other purposes without prior parental consent. However, a marketer may contact and get information from a child for the purpose of obtaining parental consent.

Marketers should not collect, without prior parental consent, personally identifiable information online from children that would permit any off-line contact with the child or distribute to third parties, without prior parental consent, information collected from a child that would permit any contact with that child. Reasonable steps to prevent the online publication or posting of information that would allow a third party to contact a child off-line unless the marketer has prior parental consent.

Marketers should not entice a child to divulge personal identifiable information by the prospect of a special game, prize or other offer nor should they make a child's access to a web site contingent on the collection of personal information. Only online contact information used to enhance the interactivity of the site is permitted. The following assumptions underlie these online guidelines:

When a marketer directs a site at a certain age group, it can expect that the visitors to that site are in that age range; and when a marketer asks the age of the child, the marketer can assume the answer to be truthful.

Marketing Ethics:

Ethical behavior and corporate stewardship are long-standing issues at every level of the business organization. While the mass media would have us believe that ethical misdeeds and malfeasance are the spawn of corporate executives and some board members, the real problem starts in the guts of organizations – often in marketing. Some of our marketing executive friends won't like this discussion.

Conflict Foundations

Marketing managers, sales executives, field operatives, category managers and market analysts are all presented with some level of conflict in their everyday work of generating revenue, serving customers, growing brand and market equity, managing profit levels and capital levels, etc. Several factors shape the behaviors, activities and successes of these people.

People in marketing, sales and service functions are faced with the conflicting pressures of generating results and serving the customer. There are unique timing and resource issues on the table, and these are often shaped by financial incentives at different levels of the buy-sell relationship. These conditions set the stage for ethnical, economic and lapses in business character.

Part of the ethical standards and principles platform starts with the character of the people and the character baked into their leaders. Another part of the equation is the inherent structural challenge that is posed when the direct and indirect incentives of the organization provide the latitude to "say one thing and do another" in reference to ethical standards, behaviors and response.

Effective Leadership in Marketing Model

Since the dawn of the industrial age, business leaders and stakeholders have sought to define meaningful business goals. The common starting point in most entities is the creation of strategic and economic value and return on business assets. Beyond this, however, setting meaningful business goals takes on more important issues like what the company stands for, where it's headed and what makes it perform. These ideas set the expectations for the entire organization. This is where the four natural goals of business come into the management equation. Every company has some version of these natural

goals – expressed in different ways, and influenced by behaviors throughout the organization.

1. *Competitive Advantage...Fundamental Differentiation*
2. *Economic Performance...Economic Value and Risk*
3. *Customer Connection...Attracting and Sustaining*
4. *Corporate Stewardship...Stakeholder Considerations*

In some organizations, these goals are defined very specifically and expressed very forcefully in the context of strategy. In other organizations, they're implied in general statements, actions and performance measures. Rarely are they ignored. We see these four natural goals of business in vision statements and strategic plans; also in balanced scorecards and performance dashboards, albeit in different forms. The approach favors

the clarification of the four natural goals in company-specific terms for

planning and leadership purposes. The intent and impact of efforts tied to

these natural goals will change in response to dynamic business

conditions. That adds to the importance of active review and goal

assessment:

1.   Position and Market Category Leverage –

       Companies with distinctive edge and strength in a market

       category create more economic value.

2.   Competence and Strategic Resources Advantage –

       Companies with unique technical, marketing, operating

       and network assets create more economic value.

Both ideas make sense, and they are part of the mix in every

company. They are the basis for generating profitable, sustainable,

capital-efficient business growth and evolution. They relate to all four natural goals, and they power the engines that drive overall business results in every kind of company.

Exclusive Goals and Imperatives

Academics and consultants often debate the merits of so-called core strategy models like customer centricity, cost leadership, category innovation, and operational edge. Some suggest that a company must choose one path, and one core strategy commitment. In some business sectors, they may be

right. It can be very difficult to address innovative customer approaches while the organization attempts to screw down operating costs and assets here is where the integrity of the company is spotlighted. Research strongly suggests that better companies have a cogent approach to targeting their market,   while leveraging simultaneous efforts for operational efficiency without compromising company standards and integrity.

Can a company with a bent for innovation also be a company that has an acute sense of cost and asset leverage? Yes, indeed, and there is plenty of evidence that better companies do this every day.

Natural Goals in More Detail

The power and purpose of the natural goals of business is clearly in the details. In the following outlines, we've attempted to capture some of the more common and practical examples of natural goals in practice. Let's look at the basic framework:

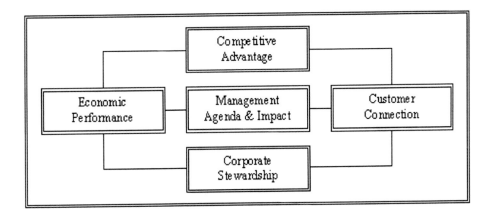

At the center of this model is the role of the management agenda. Effective Management Leadership in marketing, and the intended impact of the company's natural goals. The *agenda* is the focus of plans and actions. The *impact* is the combined result of business strategy and behavior. The four natural goals of business are linked in the management agenda and the impact evaluation process. Performance is a function of all four natural goals. They all count in the end-game of strategy management.

The following outlines represent starting points for most companies. The issues and questions that are unique to an organization can be applied and evaluated accordingly. Recommend the ongoing review of those natural goals as part of the strategic thought and leadership of the company – at every level of the business.

Competitive Advantage

There are several fundamental origins of competitive advantage. These include better products and services, better operating resources and processes, better talent and organization, better technical assets and capacity, better access to markets, etc. Some would suggest that competitive advantage is the result of clever business definition, savvy marketing approach and productivity. The principal issues that bring business definition and productivity together include:

- *Product and Service Scope*

- *Market and Customer Focus*

- *Resource and Network Assets*

These elements represent the platform for creating strategic and economic value, and in any given market sector, one company is fundamentally more productive than the rest. Business definition, value proposition, category management and resource management are important issues in competitive edge.

Economic Performance

The relevance of economic performance is obvious. Companies must generate revenue, margins, operating cash flow and asset leverage, or they cannot create real economic value. Economic performance is most often gauged in terms of:

- *Revenue and Margin Dynamics*

- *Expense and Asset Dynamics*

- *Cash Flow Behavior and Risk*

Companies can develop and track a wide range of financial measures that are useful in gauging economic performance. Often, these metrics are helpful in understanding the current and emergent profit impact of strategy management. These economic resources are relevant at every level of the organization, because people at every level impact the performance of the business as a whole. We advocate for the "cascading" of specific economic metrics for planning with governance, general management and the broader organization.

Customer Connection

Over the last 20+ years, we've seen an explosion in the methods and resources for getting close to the customer in terms of market information, marketing systems, customer support and more advanced customer relationship solutions. This wave of effort in customer connectivity is focused on:

- *Enhanced Customer Attraction*

- *Enhanced Customer Retention*

- *Economic Value of Customers*

Customer-centric ideas have been part of the marketing thought and language for 80+ years. The challenge in the context of the natural goals of business is to connect the company more productively with the right customers...customers that make sense for the business model. Customer connectivity has important supply chain and demand chain strategy implications, and it has key profit implications.

Corporate Stewardship

The integrity and cultural standards of an organization have a lot to do with its performance. In the context of the natural goals of business, corporate stewardship means focusing on stakeholder issues that are right for the company:

- *Employee and Talent Assets*

- *General Business Relationships*

- *Community Considerations*

Corporate stewardship can be expressed from many different platforms. Some companies operate with well-established standards of citizenship and stewardship. Others are dependent on broader ethical principles and boundaries. And then, of course, some companies have serious voids with respect to integrity, citizenship and legitimacy, and this often leads to disaster.

Managing a Blended Approach

The premise of natural goals is derived from the experience of companies that have attempted to balance their focus on four complementary business ideas and strategic ideals. These companies assume that economic performance is a function of doing the right things in corporate stewardship, customer connection and competitive advantage. They understand the inter-relatedness of these four natural goals.

To bring about this kind of balance, senior executives and directors need to construct a sense of inter-relatedness. Healthcare companies are trumpeting a no margin – no mission theme. Automotive companies are learning the importance of growing integrated supply chain relationships for competitive edge. Technology suppliers are learning the relevance of customer value propositions that support smart, faster application development. These reflect the press for blended ideas.

Business Evolution and Dynamics

What happens when the conditions of a market category change in material ways? Can a company anticipate, act and develop its approach to conditions? The answers to these questions should reflect the management of natural goals.   It is suggested that leaders look at things through this lens:

Today's Orientation	Natural Goals	Tomorrow's Issues
	Competitive Advantage	
	Economic Performance	
	Customer Connections	
	Corporate Stewardships	

Dewar Sloan, Marketing Design Leaders has   tracked the business debate on corporate objectives and natural goals for more than 25 years. What moved this team to conduct further research on this subject was the prevalence of superficial vision statements and the problems associated with framing meaningful business goals that tied together the expectations, behaviors and performance of the 21st century business organization. In framing the four natural goals of business, they seek to raise the questions that will help guide leaders at every level of an organization toward greater performance and ethical planning.   (Wolfe, Daniel 2004).

Conclusion: Leadership Assets Redefined for Marketing

Leadership has been defined in many different frameworks since the dawn of human history. There is significant depth in the research literature on the elements and attributes of leadership. There is similar depth in the popular culture of business leadership, focusing on the practical meaning and themes of leadership. We look at leadership effectiveness in marketing as a function of three important components of a framework. These are *competence, character and connection.*

These components and their interactions make up the essential pieces and parts of the marketing leadership equation. Senior managers, as well as sales and marketing operations agree on these elements and their relevance in business.

Exploring the Four Dimensions of Marketing Leadership:

Leadership happens through human thought and behavior at four different levels or dimensions of an organization. These four leadership dimensions include:

1. *Individual and Self-Level Leadership*

2. *Group and Functional-Level Leadership*

3. *Cross Function and Process-Level Leadership*

4. *Cross Boundary and Network-Level Leadership*

One of the greatest challenges in leadership development is to attract, cultivate and sustain great talent in all four dimensions of leadership. The challenge is to find the meaning and match of these four dimensions of marketing leadership.

Getting Down to the Specific Elements

Here we have the framework that supports marketing leadership analysis and planning. This framework is built upon a series of 15 important and sometimes provocative ideas. These ideas are posed in the form of review and audit questions, and they are supported by a short series of thought-starters for discussion. The discussion about leadership effectiveness and development in marketing can take place in routine departmental planning, or in the context of a more dedicated and focused assessment program. Either way, the framework is the same, and the central question about marketing leadership usually comes down to this: Do we have effective marketing leadership in each of the four dimensions of organizational activity?

For most marketing organizations, these are significant and often perplexing issues. Marketing is a complex and dynamic frontier for companies in every sector. Developing the four Dimensions of Leadership in Marketing is one of the most critical aspects of organization development. The following outline focuses on leadership thought and behavior issues in all four dimensions.

Most companies that engage in a detailed assessment of these leadership components and dimensions are pleased to find that the effort is worthwhile in several ways. First, it presents **the language** for discussion on a subject that is often passed over as a development subject. Second, it provides **the constructs** for dealing with specific issues and opportunities in building more effective leaderships in marketing. Third, it presents **the pathways** for improving the performance of the entire organization, not just in marketing.

Suggestions for application of this framework begin with a review of marketing strategy and management conditions, referencing specific objectives, challenges, principles, and business priorities. Next, lay out the functions and processes of marketing as defined in formal organizational structure, process management disciplines, process improvement programs, and informal "white space" on the organization chart. Be sure to include all direct and indirect functions that touch the customer. Next, plug in some general preference ratings for leadership assets that seem appropriate for each function or process, at each dimension of the organization. As a specific example, what kind of leadership assets do we need for our product managers as they operate individually and across the organization? Complete general preference ratings for each function and process, generate some general performance ratings for the organization, using input from the people who operate in and around these roles. 360° assessments, manager assessments or variations on talent development reviews can provide the input data for general performance ratings. Some kind of 360° assessment is useful in shaping measures of each function or process, at each level of the organization and beyond the boundaries where applicable.

A given preference ratings indicate what managers and incumbents consider ideal for the position. The general performance ratings indicate what managers and incumbents view as their current reality. Getting the right talent on board is obviously a critical step toward marketing effectiveness. Developing talent to align with strategy and structure is part of the job for leaders at every

level of the company. Developing talent as a cultural and competitive resource is
one of the key platforms in companies that thrive on so called hidden assets.
Those companies create new strategic, ethical and economic value in some
profoundly important ways, competing with capability in:

- *Better, Smarter, Faster Product Marketing Programs*
- *More Profitable Brand and Category Pricing Models*
- *Greater Access to Customers, Upstream and Downstream*
- *Better Leverage with Supply and Demand Chain Partners*
- *More Specific Knowledge of Customer Needs and Behavior*
- *Better Sense of Category Trends and Opportunity Fronts*

These are some of the implications of effective leadership in marketing.
There are other benefits including the ability to attract good people to the
organization, and the ability to develop senior management and staff resources.
Developing the Four Dimensions of Leadership in Marketing is part of a
broader agenda for strategy management and leadership development.
Through research and planning the focus on the practical drivers of business
model success and organizational resolve to perform in turbulent markets.
Companies are dynamic and evolutionary entities. More than ever, companies

and their stakeholders need effective leadership, especially in marketing
strategy and management.

ETHICAL AND MORAL PRINCIPLES

The Second Vatican Council declared: "If the media are to be
correctly employed, it is essential that all who use them know the
principles of the moral order and apply them faithfully in this domain." The
moral order to which this refers is the order of the law of human nature,
binding upon all because it is "written on their hearts" (*Rom.* 2:15) and
embodies the imperatives of authentic human fulfillment. For Christians,
moreover, the law of human nature has a deeper dimension, a richer
meaning. "Christ is the 'Beginning' who, having taken on human nature,
definitively illumines it in its constitutive elements and in its dynamism of
charity towards God and neighbor." Here we comprehend the deepest
significance of human freedom: that it makes possible an authentic moral
response, in light of Jesus Christ, to the call "to form our conscience, to
make it the object of a continuous conversion to what is true and to what is
good."

In this context, the media of social communications have two options,
and only two. Either they help human persons to grow in their

understanding and practice of what is true and good, or they are destructive forces in conflict with human well being. That is entirely true of advertising. Against this background, then, we point to this fundamental principle for people engaged in advertising: advertisers — that is, those who commission, prepare or disseminate advertising — are morally responsible for what they seek to move people to do; and this is a responsibility also shared by publishers, broadcasting executives, and others in the communications world, as well as by those who give commercial or political endorsements, to the extent that they are involved in the advertising process.

If an instance of advertising seeks to move people to choose and act rationally in morally good ways that are of true benefit to themselves and others, persons involved in it do what is morally good; if it seeks to move people to do evil deeds that are self-destructive and destructive of authentic community, they do evil.

This applies also to the means and the techniques of advertising - it is morally wrong to use manipulative, exploitative, corrupt and corrupting methods of persuasion and motivation. In this regard, we note special problems associated with so-called indirect advertising that attempts to move people to act in certain ways — for example, purchase particular products — without their being fully aware that they are being swayed. The techniques involved here include showing certain products or forms of behavior in superficially glamorous settings associated with superficially glamorous people; in extreme cases, it may even involve the use of subliminal messages.

Within this very general framework, we can identify several moral principles that are particularly relevant to advertising and can focus on three:

    a) Truthfulness

    b) The dignity of the human person

    c) Social responsibility

a) Truthfulness in Advertising

Even today, some advertising is simply and deliberately untrue. Generally speaking, though, the problem of truth in advertising is somewhat more subtle: it is not that advertising says what is overtly false, but that it can distort the truth by implying things that are not so or withholding relevant facts. As Pope John Paul II points out, on both the individual and social levels, truth and freedom are inseparable; without truth as the basis, starting point and criterion of discernment, judgment, choice and action, there can be no authentic exercise of freedom. The Catechism of the Catholic Church, quoting the Second Vatican Council, insists that the content of communication be "true and — within the limits set by justice and charity — complete"; the content should, moreover, be communicated "honestly and properly."

To be sure, advertising, like other forms of expression, has its own conventions and forms of stylization, and these must be taken into account when discussing truthfulness. People take for granted some rhetorical and symbolic exaggeration in advertising; within the limits of recognized and accepted practice, this can be allowable. But it is a fundamental principle that advertising may not deliberately seek to deceive, whether it does that by what it says, by what it implies, or by what it fails to say. "The proper exercise of the right to information demands that the content of what is communicated be true and, within the limits set by justice and charity, complete. .. Included here is the obligation to avoid any manipulation of truth for any reason."

b) *The Dignity of the Human Person*

There is an "imperative requirement" that advertising "respect the human person, his right to make a responsible choice, his interior freedom; all these goods would be violated if man's lower inclinations were to be exploited, or his capacity to reflect and decide compromised. These abuses are not merely hypothetical possibilities but realities in much advertising today. Advertising can violate the dignity of the human person both through its content — what is advertised, the manner in which it is advertised — and through the impact it seeks to make upon its audience. We have spoken already of such things as appeals to lust, vanity, envy and greed, and of techniques that manipulate and exploit human weakness. In such circumstances, advertisements readily become "vehicles of a deformed outlook on life, on the family, on religion and on morality — an outlook that does not respect the true dignity and destiny of the human person."

This problem is especially acute where particularly vulnerable groups or classes of persons are concerned: children and young people, the elderly, the poor, the culturally disadvantaged and people with self-esteem issues. Much advertising directed at children apparently tries to exploit their credulity and suggestibility, in the hope that they will put pressure on their parents to buy products of no real benefit to them. Advertising like this offends against the dignity and rights of both children and parents; it intrudes upon the parent-child relationship and seeks to manipulate it to its own base ends. Also, some of the comparatively little advertising directed specifically to the elderly or culturally disadvantaged seems designed to play upon their fears so as to persuade them to allocate some of their limited resources to goods or services of dubious value.

c) Advertising and Social Responsibility

Social responsibility is such a broad concept that we can note here only a few of the many issues and concerns relevant under this heading to the question of advertising. The ecological issue is one. Advertising that fosters a lavish life style which wastes resources and despoils the environment offends against important ecological concerns. In his desire to have and to enjoy rather than to be and grow, man consumes the resources of the earth and his own life in an excessive and disordered way. Man thinks that he can make arbitrary use of the earth, subjecting it without restraint to his will, as though it did not have its own requisites and a prior God-given purpose, which man can indeed develop but must not betray.

As this suggests, something more fundamental is at issue here: authentic and integral human development. Advertising that reduces human progress to acquiring material goods and cultivating a lavish life style expresses a false, destructive vision of the human person harmful to individuals and society alike. When people fail to practice "a rigorous respect for the moral, cultural and spiritual requirements, based on the dignity of the person and on the proper identity of each community, beginning with the family and religious societies," then even material abundance and the conveniences that technology makes available "will prove unsatisfying and in the end contemptible." Advertisers, like people engaged in other forms of social communication, have a serious duty to express and foster an authentic vision of human development in its material, cultural and spiritual dimensions. Communication that meets this standard is, among other things, a true expression of solidarity. Indeed, the two things — communication and solidarity — are inseparable, because, as the *Catechism of the Catholic Church* points out, solidarity is "a consequence of genuine and right communication and the free circulation of ideas that further knowledge and respect for others."

CONCLUSION: ETHICAL AND MORAL PRINCIPLES

The indispensable guarantors of ethically correct behavior by the advertising industry are the well formed and responsible consciences of advertising professionals themselves: consciences sensitive to their duty not merely to serve the interests of those who commission and finance their work but also to respect and uphold the rights and interests of their audiences and to serve the common good.

Many women and men professionally engaged in advertising do have sensitive consciences, high ethical standards and a strong sense of responsibility. But even for them external pressures — from the clients who commission their work as well as from the competitive internal dynamics of their profession — can create powerful inducements to unethical behavior. That underlines the need for external structures and systems to support and encourage responsible practice in advertising and to discourage the irresponsible.

Voluntary ethical codes are one such source of support. These already exist in a number of places. Welcome as they are, though, they are only as effective as the willingness of advertisers to comply strictly with them. It is up to the directors and managers of the media which carry advertising to make known to the public, to subscribe to and to apply the codes of professional ethics which already have been opportunely established so as to have the cooperation of the public in making these codes still better and in enforcing their observance.

We emphasize the importance of public involvement. Representatives of the public should participate in the formulation, application and periodic updating of ethical codes. The public representatives should include ethicists and church people, as well as representatives of consumer groups. Individuals do well to organize themselves into such groups in order to protect their interests in relation to commercial interests.

Public authorities also have a role to play. On the one hand, government should not seek to control and dictate policy to the advertising industry, any more than to other sectors of the communications media. On the other hand, the regulation of advertising content and practice, already existing in many places, can and should extend beyond banning false advertising, narrowly defined. "By promulgating laws and overseeing their application, public authorities should ensure that public morality and social progress are not gravely endangered ' through misuse of the media."

For example, government regulations should address such questions as the quantity of advertising, especially in broadcast media, as well as the content of advertising directed at groups particularly vulnerable to exploitation, such as children and old people. Political advertising also seems an appropriate area for regulation: how much may be spent, how and from whom may money for advertising be raised, etc.

The media of news and information should make it a point to keep the public informed about the world of advertising. Considering advertising's social impact, it is appropriate that media regularly review and critique the performance of advertisers, just as they do other groups whose activities have a significant influence on society. Besides using media to evangelize, the Church for her part needs to grasp the full implications of the observation by Pope John Paul: that media comprise a central part of that great modern "Areopagus" where ideas are shared and attitudes and values are formed. This points to a "deeper reality" than simply using media to spread the Gospel message, important as that is. "It is also necessary to integrate that message into the 'new culture' created by modern communications" with its new ways of communicating... new languages, new techniques and a new psychology.

In light of this insight, it is important that media education be part of pastoral planning and a variety of pastoral and educational programs carried on by the Church, including Catholic schools. This includes education regarding the role of advertising in today's world and its relevance to the work of the Church. Such education should seek to prepare people to be informed and alert in their approach to advertising as to other forms of communication. As the *Catechism of the Catholic Church* points out, "the means of social communication. ... can give rise to a certain passivity among users, making them less than vigilant consumers of what is said or shown. Users should practice moderation and discipline in their approach to the mass media." (Foley, Pastoro, 1997)

In the final analysis, however, where freedom of speech and communication exists, it is largely up to advertisers themselves to ensure ethically responsible practices in their profession. Besides avoiding abuses, advertisers should also undertake to repair the harm sometimes done by advertising, insofar as that is possible: for example, by publishing corrective notices, compensating injured parties, increasing the quantity of public service advertising, and the like. This question of 'reparations' is a matter of legitimate involvement not only by industry self-regulatory bodies and public interest groups, but also by public authorities. Where unethical practices have become widespread and entrenched, conscientious advertisers may be called upon to make significant personal sacrifices to correct them. But people who want to do what is morally right must always be ready to suffer loss and personal injury rather than to do what is wrong. This is a duty for Christians, followers of Christ, certainly; but not only for them. "In this witness to the absoluteness of the moral good Christians are not alone: they are supported by the moral sense present in peoples and by the great religious and sapiential traditions of East and West.

We do not wish, and certainly we do not expect, to see advertising eliminated from the contemporary world. Advertising is an important element in today's society, especially in the functioning of a market economy, which is becoming more and more widespread. Moreover, for the reasons and in the ways sketched here, we believe advertising can, and often does, play a constructive role in economic growth, in the exchange of information and ideas, and in the fostering of solidarity among individuals and groups. Yet it also can do, and often does, grave harm to individuals and to the common good. In light of these reflections, therefore, we call upon advertising professionals and upon all those involved in the process of commissioning and disseminating advertising to eliminate its socially harmful aspects and observe high ethical standards in regard to truthfulness, human dignity and social responsibility. In this way, they will make a special and significant contribution to human

progress and to the common good.

REFERENCES

Arndorfer, James B. "Kraft's Pizza Unit Faces Freezer Burn: Food Maker Needs New Products to Fire Up Former Growth Business," Crain's Chicago Business, 19 Jan. 2004. 3, 26.

Arndorfer, James B. "Oreo Woes Bringing Kraft Down: Fat Fears," Advertising Age, 5. Jan 2004. 4,32.

Atkinson, Claire. "Coke Catapults Starcom Media Vest," Advertising Age, 9 Feb. 2004. S-6, S10, S14.

American Academy of Pediatrics. Prevention of Pediatric Overweight and Obesity: American Academy of Pediatrics Policy Statement; Organizational Principles to Guide and Define the Child Health System and/or Improve the Health of All Children; Committee on Nutrition. Pediatrics. 2003;112:424-430

Banis HT, Varni JW, Wallander JL, Korsch BM, Jay SM, Adler R, Garcia-Temple E, & Negrete V. Psychological and social adjustment of obese children and their families. Child: Care, Health, and Development. 1998;14,157-173.

Barker M. Birthweight and body fat distribution in adolescent girls. Arch Dis Child 1997; 77(5): 381-383.

Barlow SE, & Dietz WH. Obesity evaluation and treatment: Expert
Committee recommendations. Pediatrics, 1998; 102(3):
URL:http://www.pediatrics.org/cgi/content/full/102/3/e29.

Bodo Schlegelmilch , Marketing Ethics: An International Perspective,
London : International Business Press, 1998

Bouchard C and Perusse L. Heredity and body fat. Annual Review of
Nutrition, 1988;8:259-77.

Black, Lisa and Vogt, Amanda; "Events Teaching Teens Valuable, but
Painful Lessons." Chicago Tribune. 11 Sept. 2003.

Carroll, Archie B, Business and Society - Ethics and Stakeholder
Management, South-Western Publishing Co, USA, 1993

Center for A New American Dream. "Kids and Commercialism: 2001.
25 March 2004. www.newdream.org/campaign/kids/facts.html

Chang, Anita. "Setting Curfews for Teens," Associated Press, 17 September
2004.

Cook, Guy. Discourse of Advertising, 2nd ed. London - New York:
Routledge   2001.

Condor, Bob. "Hope Grows Along with Food in Pioneer's Urban Farming Projects," Chicago Tribune, 14 Mar 2004. 8.

Crane, Andrew. Marketing, Morality & The Natural Environment. New York - London: Routledge, 2001.

Direct Marketing Ethics Association. Feb. 2004. www.the-dma.org.

Eckel, Robert H. M.D. "The Deadly Domino Effect: Obesity, Diabetes, Heart Disease," 16 Feb. 2004, A3

Feuer, Jack. "Big Is Beautiful: Junk Food Marketers Aren't Criminals. Get off Their Back," Adweek, 15 Dec. 2003. 18.

Foley, John P. and Pierfranco, Pastore. Feast of the Choir. Rome, Vatican Publications, 1997.

Fox, Warwick. Ethics and the Built Environment. Conneticut: Greenwood 1997.

Garfield, Bob. "Pepsi Finally Acknowledges Real Point of Cola in New Ads", Advertising Age, 1 Dec. 2003. 37.

Goldberg, Nieca, M.D. "Women & Heart Disease," Time Magazine, 16 Feb. 2004. A1.

Greenberg, Karl, "BMW Meets MTV in X3 Launch Campaign: Targets Twenty-somethings," Adweek, 15, Dec. 2003 6.

Halliday, Jean, "Volvo Goes After Younger Buyers," Advertising Age, 26, 2004. 8

Hoffmann, W. M. & J.M. Moore, Business Ethics - Reading and Cases in Corporate Morality, McGraw-Hill, 1990.

Huxley, Aldous. Brave New World Revisited, Chapter VI - The Arts of Selling). New York. 1998.

Jacobs, Alice K. M.D.   "Reventing Heart Disease: The Journey to a Healthy Heart Starts with the First Step," 16 Feb 2004. A2.

J.R. Boatright Ethics and the Conduct of Business, Englewood Cliffs, N.J.: Prentice Hall, 1993. (pp1-117)

Klein, Sarah. "Weight Watchers," Crain's Chicago Business, 22 Dec. 2003 13, 15.

Lee, Chin-Chuan. Power, Money and Media: Communication Patterns and Bureaucratic Control in China.   (State): NW Univ. Press 2000.

Lung, Shirley, "Despite Best Efforts, Doughnut Makers Must Fry, Fry Again,

The Wall Street Journal, 5 Jan. 2004 Vol. CCXLIII No. 2 - A 1, A12.

Lippert, Barbara. "Sizzle and Fizzle,"   ADWEEK, 22 Dec. 2003. 12-14.

MacArthur, Kate, "McD's Sees Growth, But Are Ads a Factor?" Advertising

Age, 24 Nov. 2003. 3

MacArthur, Kate. "Coke Sets It's Sights on Teens With Mall Red Lounges,"

Advertising Age, 15, Dec. 2003. 4.

      "Low Carb Bandwagon: Fast-Feeders ditch buns to lure dieters,"

        Advertising Age, 12 Jan. 2004. 3, 39.

MacArthur, Kate and Neff, Jack. "Sprite Shifts Gears In Quest for Street

Cred," (1, 3, 29); "What's Eating Burger King: Brand Problems Youth

Appeal," (30), Advertising Age, 26, Jan. 2004

McMains, Andrew. "Viewers Decide Content on RCN's New Cable

Channel," Adweek, 15, Dec. 2003   14

Madden, Normandy. "Chinese Youth Aren't Patriotic Purchasers: Most

Favor Coke and Nike,"   Advertising Age, 5 Jan. 2005. 6.

Madden, Normandy. "Cellphones to Add Cartoon Characters: Youth

Marketing," Advertising Age, 10 Nov. 2003. 16.

Marconi, Joe. Future Marketing: Targeting Seniors, Boomers and

Generation X and Y.   USA: McGraw-Hill Trade 2000.

Marcus, Judy. "Taking It Off," North Shore Magazine, April 2004, 42-47

Marketing Ethics and Social Responsibility. 2000. DePaul University. 3 Mar

2004.   http://condo.depaul.edu/ethics/bizethics.html ;

http://college.hmco.com/Prind/Ferr/chap3b.html

Martin, Andrew. "Critics: Obesity Fight Starved for Cash, Food Advertising

Dwarfs Nutrition Promotion," Chicago Tribune, 14 Mar 2004. 9.

Masterson, Kathryn, "No Supersize For You," <u>RedEye Newspaper,</u> 3 Mar. 2003, p 1, 8.

Moses, Lucia. "Kneeling to Young Continues: Hot Summer Turns Cool," Editor & Publisher, 11 Aug. 2003. 7

N.A.S.O. "North American Association for the Study of Obesity." 2003-2004. <u>www.obesityresearch.org</u>.

Neff, Jack. "P&G Tests Revival of Eagle Snacks Brand: Chip War," <u>Advertising Age</u>, 5 Jan. 2004. 3,22.

<u>Overweight and Obesity: What You Can Do</u>. 2001. Surgeon General's Call to Action. 14 Apr. 2004; <u>www.surgeongeneral.gov/topics/obesity/calltoaction/fact_whatcanyoudo.ht</u> <u>m</u>

Parsa, Faramarz and Lankford, William H. : "Business Students' Views of Ethics," 1998. Richards College of Business, University of West Georgia. 2 Apr. 2004. <u>www.westga.edu/~bquest/1998/ethics.html</u>.

"Pepsi Trades in Joy for Focus on Cola", <u>Advertising Age</u>, 10 Nov. 2003.
14.

Phillips, Michael J. <u>Ethics & Manipulation in Advertising: Answering a</u>
<u>Flawed Indictment.</u> Conneticut: Greenwood Pub. Group 1997.

Phillips, Michaael J. <u>Marketing Withoug Advertising: Inspire Customers to</u>
<u>Rave About Your Business & Create Lassting Success</u>. 4th ed. California:
Nolo 2003.

Richards, Jef I. "Advertising Law & Ethics. Department of Advertising,
The University of Texas at Austin. 3 Mar. 2004.
<u>http://advertising.utexas.edu/research/law/index.html</u>

Rozhorn, Tracie, "Student Chic is Remaking Itself, Trading Grunge for
Cable Knit." <u>New York Times</u>. 16, August 2004.

Sims, Ronald R. <u>Teaching Business Ethics for Effective Learning</u>.
(State): Greenwood Publising Group. 2002 .
Stein, Joel. "Paging Dr. Fatkins." <u>Time Magazine</u>, 23, Jan. 2004, 37.

Stone, Merlin. <u>Successful Customer Relationship Marketing: New</u>

<u>Thinking, New Strategies, New Tools for Getting Closer to Your</u>

<u>Customers</u>. Connecticut: Kogan Page 2001.

Thompson, Stephanie,. "Kellogg Bulls Its Way into Fruit Snacks" -

"General Mills Bows First Protein Cereal: New Total Extension Aimed At

Appealing to low-carb dieters," <u>Advertising Age</u>, 9 Feb. 2004. 3, 53.

" Low-carb Craze Blitzes Food Biz," <u>Advertising Age</u>, 5 Jan. 2004.

1, 22,

"Weight-Loss Programs Counter Low-Carb Diets," <u>Advertising</u>

<u>Age</u>, 5 Jan.   2004. 22.

Tribune Co. Marketing Source. 2002-2004. Intranet http:sams.ctc.com

TRU "Teenage Research Unlimited." <u>Teen Overview and Research</u>

<u>Studies</u>. March 2004 <u>www.teenresearch.com/view</u>

Teinowitz, Ira. "Marketers Blast Charges In Alcohol Suit: Refute Idea They

Go After Teens," <u>Advertising Age</u>, 1 Dec. 2003. 10.

Weil, Elizabeth. "Geared Up For Health," <u>Time Magazine</u> March 2004.

Bonus insert.

<u>Welcome to Burn the Fat</u>. 2003 "Overweight and Obesity". 25 Mar 2004.

<u>www.burn-the-fat.com/home.html</u>

Winslow, Ron, "Researchers Link Sharp Rise in Disability Rates for

Younger Adults to Obesity," <u>Wall Street Journal</u>, 9 Jan. 2004. A7, A9.

Wolf, Daniel. <u>Dewar Sloan Consultants and Advisors</u>.

www.dewarsloan.com Version 02/2004.

Zollo, Peter. "When Marketing to Teens, Trends Live Fast, Die Young,"

Crains Chicago Business, 16, Feb. 2004. 11

Appendix A - Media:

What Particular Area?

Newspaper: 9/12/24 county areas

TV: DMA (Designated Market Area)
           - 16 county area

Cable System: Service area

Radio: Metro
           - 10 county area
        TSA (Total Survey Area)
           - 48 county area

Outdoor: Location

Magazines: Circulation Area

Appendix – B: Terminology

Media Comparisons

Schedule	Newspapers Gallup, CMR & ABC/Claritas	Broadcast TV Gallup & CMR	Cable TV Gallup	Radio Media Monitor	Outdoor N/A	Magazines Gallup & CMR
Measures						
circulation						
reach	X	X	X	X	X	X
frequency	X	X	X	X	X	X
GRP	X	X	X	X	X	X
impression	X	X	X	X	X	X
CPM	X	X	X	X	X	X
CPR						
duplication	X					
spots						
DEC*					X	
traffic counts						
Showings					X	
coverage/composition						
How to Buy	section/geography	dayparts	Dayparts/Network	dayparts	Location	Audience
Geography	county 8/9/12/24 zones 4/5/6/8/9/10	DMA-17 county	service area	Metro-10 county TSA-48 county	market definition	circulation area

* DEC means Daily Effective Circulation

Broadcast TV

Schedule	Newspapers Gallup, CMR & ABC/Claritas	Broadcast TV Gallup & CMR	Cable TV Gallup	Radio Media Monitor	Outdoor N/A	Magazines Gallup & CMR
Measures						
circulation						
reach	X	X	X	X	X	X
frequency	X	X	X	X	X	X
GRP	X	X	X	X	X	X
Impression	X	X	X	X	X	X
CPM	X	X	X	X	X	X
CPR						
duplication	X					
spots						
DEC*					X	
traffic counts						
Showings					X	
coverage/ composition						
How to Buy	section/geography	dayparts	Dayparts/Network	dayparts	Location	Audience
Geography	county 8/9/12/24 zones 4/5/6/8/9/10	DMA-17 county	service area	Metro-1o county TSA-48 county	market definition	circulation area

Appendix B3:

Information Needed To
Analyze A TV Buy

■ Target Audience Definition

+ Gender   + Income

+ Age   + Other

+ Education

■ Total Delivery Goal (GRPs)

+ Overall

+ By week

■ # of Weeks On-Air

■ Daypart Mix
- % Early Morning
- % Day
- % Early Fringe
- % Early News
- % Prime Access
- % Prime
- % Late News
- % Late Fringe
- % Cable

■ Estimated Budget

Appendix B4:

Cable TV

Schedule	Newspapers Gallup, CMR & ABC/Claritas	Broadcast TV Gallup & CMR	Cable TV Gallup	Radio Media Monitor	Outdoor N/A	Magazines Gallup & CMR
Measures						
circulation						
reach	X	X	X	X	X	X
frequency	X	X	X	X	X	X
GRP	X	X	X	X	X	X
impression	X	X	X	X	X	X
CPM	X	X	X	X	X	X
CPR						
duplication	X					
spots						
DEC*					X	
traffic counts						
Showings					X	
coverage/ composition						
How to Buy	section/geography	dayparts	Dayparts/Network	dayparts	Location	Audience
Geography	county 8/9/12/24 zones 4/5/6/8/9/10	DMA-17 county	service area	Metro-10 county TSA-48 county	market definition	circulation area

Appendix B 5:

Radio

Schedule	Newspapers Gallup, CMR & ABC/Claritas	Broadcast TV Gallup & CMR	Cable TV Gallup	Radio Media Monitor	Outdoor N/A	Magazines Gallup & CMR
Measures						
circulation						
reach	X	X	X	X	X	X
frequency	X	X	X	X	X	X
GRP	X	X	X	X	X	X
impression	X	X	X	X	X	X
CPM	X	X	X	X	X	X
CPR						
duplication	X					
spots						
DEC*					X	
traffic counts						
Showings					X	
coverage/ composition						
How to Buy	section/geography	dayparts	Dayparts/Network	dayparts	Location	Audience
Geography	county 8/9/12/24 zones 4/5/6/8/9/10	DMA-17 county	service area	Metro-10 county TSA-48 county	market definition	circulation area

Appendix 6:

Outdoor

Schedule	Newspapers Gallup, CMR & ABC/Claritas	Broadcast TV Gallup & CMR	Cable TV Gallup	Radio Media Monitor	Outdoor N/A	Magazines Gallup & CMR
Measures						
circulation						
reach	X	X	X	X	X	X
frequency	X	X	X	X	X	X
GRP	X	X	X	X	X	X
impression	X	X	X	X	X	X
CPM	X	X	X	X	X	X
CPR						
duplication	X					
spots						
DEC*					X	
traffic counts						
Showings					X	
coverage/ composition						
How to Buy	section/geography	dayparts	Dayparts/Network	dayparts	Location	Audience
Geography	county 8/9/12/24 zones 4/5/6/8/9/10	DMA-17 county	service area	Metro-10 county TSA-48 county	market definition	circulation area

Appendix B7:

Magazines

Schedule	Newspapers Gallup, CMR & ABC/Claritas	Broadcast TV Gallup & CMR	Cable TV Gallup	Radio Media Monitor	Outdoor N/A	Magazines Gallup & CMR
Measures						
circulation						
reach	X	X	X	X	X	X
frequency	X	X	X	X	X	X
GRP	X	X	X	X	X	X
impression	X	X	X	X	X	X
CPM	X	X	X	X	X	X
CPR						
duplication	X					
spots						
DEC*					X	
traffic counts						
Showings					X	
coverage/ composition						
How to Buy	section/geography	dayparts	Dayparts/Network	dayparts	Location	Audience
Geography	county 8/9/12/24 zones 4/5/6/8/9/10	DMA-17 county	service area	Metro-10 county TSA-48 county	market definition	circulation area

DEC means Daily Effective Circulation

Media Strengths & Weakness

Appendix C 1:

Newspapers

Advantages

- **History:** One of the oldest and most highly regarded media in the U.S.
- **Loyal Readers:** Enjoy a high degree of familiarity, acceptance, credibility and respect, it is a paid medium with high loyalty.
- **Mass Audience:** Newspapers reach a relatively large mass audience throughout the market with a single exposure.
- **Ad Variety:** The medium offers a variety of ad sizes that allows advertisers to meet their budgetary constraints.
- **In-Depth:** Newspaper ads have the ability to communicate lengthy, complex, or detailed information and descriptions.
- **Ease of Tracking:** It's relatively easy to track responses, primarily through couponing.
- **Lead Time:** You can place orders and copy with a relatively short lead time.
- **Exposure:** The reader controls the amount of exposure to a given ad.
- **Ad Acceptance:** Readers go to the newspaper looking for advertising

Disadvantages

- **Decreasing Penetration:** In some markets circulation is less than 50% of all households.
- **Readers don't see all ads:** Most people do not read all sections of the paper every day. An ad placed in a specific section reaches only the people who look at that section.
- **Declining Couponing:** Despite increased coupon face value, coupon redemption has been declining for years.
- **New Competition:** The classified category, as well as travel and real estate categories are under attack by the Internet.

Appendix C2:

Broadcast TV

Advantages

- **Widespread:** Over-the-air television reaches virtually all (98%) U.S. households.

- **Time Spent:** People spend a lot of time with their television sets. On average, U.S. viewers watch television more than 7 hours a day.

- **Way of Life:** Baby Boomers and Generation Xers grew up with TV.

- **Mass Exposure:** Television reaches huge mass audiences with a single exposure.

- **Sensory Appeal:** TV has the ability to grab attention and create appeal through the combination of pictures, sound and motion.

Disadvantages

- **Audience Share is Decreasing:** TV's network prime time audience has decreased dramatically, from 90% in 1980 to 43% in 1999.

- **Channel Surfing:** Requires a substantial number of spots to attain reach levels provided by one newspaper insertion.

- **Viewing Decreases as Income Increases:** U.S. adults who earn more than $60,000 watch 26% less TV than the average viewer.

- **High Production Cost:** A typical 30 second national commercial can cost hundreds of thousands of dollars to produce.

- **Restricted Viewing:** Almost all television viewing takes place in the home, making it extremely unlikely that TV advertising will influence consumers close to the point of purchase.

54

Source: Radio Advertising Bureau

Appendix C3:

Cable TV

Advantages

- **Growth Spurt:** Cable now reaches 68% of all U.S. homes.

- **Inexpensive:** Considered by many advertisers to be "discounted television".

- **Targetable:** Cable offers a considerably more targetable audience than broadcast TV.

- **Consumer Appreciation:** Most consumers like the cable they pay to receive.

- **Summer Season:** Cable's ratings typically increase during the summer, when broadcast TV ratings decline due to reruns.

Disadvantages

- **Small Audiences:** Due to so many viewing options and not all cable channels are carried by local providers, cable audiences are considerably smaller.

- **Limited Commercial Impact:** Cable still has not been invited into third of all U.S. homes.

- **Ad Clutter:** Cable carries as many 28 units of ads per hour.

- **Quality:** When local advertisers are adjacent to national sponsors, there is a need to have the same video quality as national advertisers.

Appendix C4:

Radio

Advantages

- High Frequency

- Intrusive

- Cost Effective

- Promotional Packages

- Radio is everywhere

- Can target specific audience

- Low cost in producing ad copy

- Ad copy can quickly be changed

- Radio personality give creditability to products

Disadvantages

- **Background Medium:** Listeners are not always paying full attention to what is on the radio.

- **Generates High Frequency:** Requires a substantial number of spots to attain reach levels provided by one newspaper insertion.

- **No Geographical Targetability:** Radio does not offer the ability to target a message geographically- it broadcast to everyone, everywhere.

- **Limited Opportunity to Present Detail Information:** Most commercials are only 60 seconds long, so it is difficult to present detailed, memorable information.

- **Difficult to Buy:** With more than 80 radio stations offering over 30 different formats in Chicago, it becomes difficult and expensive to buy.

- **Ad Avoidance:** Listeners change stations when commercials come on.

Appendix C5:

Outdoor

Advantages

- **Brevity:** Outdoor advertising is effective for communicating short messages or concepts.

- **Strategic Placement:** Billboards can be placed at high traffic areas or other strategic locations.

- **Attention Grabbing:** The combination of size, color and illumination attracts attention.

- **Low Cost:** Outdoor's cost-per-thousand is significantly lower than any other advertising medium.

- **Full Time Audience:** Outdoor's message appears year round, 24 hours a day.

- **Directional:** Billboards can be used as directionals, pointing out locations of a given business.

Disadvantages

- **Brevity:** Difficult to communicate product details, competitive advantages and specific consumer benefits .

- **Limited Availability:** Prime outdoor locations are often controlled by large, long-term advertisers .

- **Lack of Effective Measuring Tools:** Outdoor advertising has no truly reliable method to measure its effectiveness.

- **Low Recall:** Drivers are exposed briefly to outdoor messages, minimizing message impact and recall.

- **Ugly Image:** Due to environmental concerns, many communities have either eliminated, reduced or limited the volume and placement of billboards

- **Inflexibility:** Ads must stay up through the duration of the contract.

Appendix C6:

Magazines

Advantages

- **Readership:** According to spring 1999 Simmons data, 82%of adults 18 + say they read on or more magazines.

- **Targetability:** Specialty magazines allow advertisers to target consumers demographically, by product affinity or by lifestyle.

- **Strong Visuals:** Magazine ads can be highly creative and aesthetically appealing through the effective use of photography, graphics, color, and copy.

- **Portability:** Magazines can be carried by consumers and read almost anywhere, at any time.

- **Advertorial:** An in-depth advertising message can be created to appear more like editorial copy than an advertisement .

- **Localizing:** Regional/local editions and poly-wrap inserts offer local advertising opportunities.

Source: Radio Advertising Bureau

Disadvantages

- **Competition:** There are too many magazines and too many choices. Advertisers and consumers have over 18,000 magazines to chose from.

- **Time:** The average person spends only 5 - 6% of his or her media time reading magazines.

- **Clutter:** Magazines contain so much advertising that ad readership and recall is minimal. The typical magazine contains over 50% advertising.

- **Reach:** Due to diverse readership and consumer readership behavior , most magazines miss most of their target audience.

- **Inflexible:** Due to lead time, advertising must be prepared long before publication dates, prohibiting advertisers from responding instantly to changing market conditions.

- **Expensive:** Increased distribution and reproduction costs have forced magazines' cost-per-thousand to almost double in the past ten years. [58]

Appendix C 7:

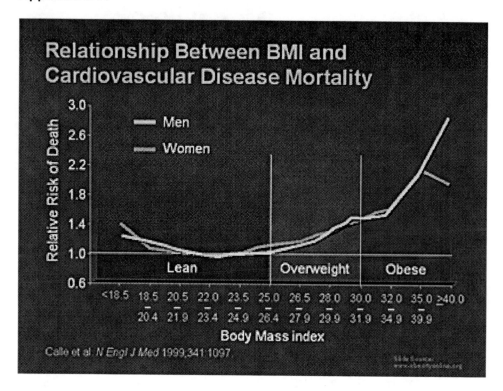

Appendix C8

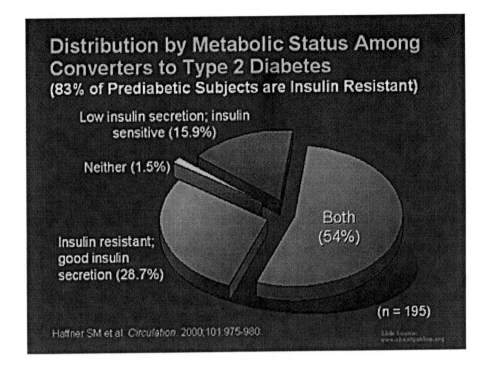

About The Author

Dr. Ileen E. Kelly, dedicated family member, educator, mentor, a twenty-nine year employee with the Chicago Tribune Newspaper; and instructor with the City College's Continuing Adult Education programs.

This author learned at the hands of masters the skills it takes to be considered a partner to the advertisers and an asset to the company. This author is committed to continuing her education and developing her teaching and mentoring skills.

Authors Early Works: "Home Work – Technology Revolutionizing the Cottage Industry," (1984). "The African American Woman – Lost in Corporate America." (1985). "Advertising vs. Marketing, The Ethical Challenge" – is this authors second business reference sources.

Printed in the United States
81294LV00003B/26